D1595777

CRUDE
BLESSINGS

CRUDE
BLESSINGS

The Amazing Life Story of
GLENN PATTERSON
American Oilman

T. M. "ROE" PATTERSON

FOREWORD BY CLOYCE TALBOTT, FORMER CEO PATTERSON–UTI ENERGY, INC.

TMP COMPANIES, INC. | FORT WORTH, TX

Published by
TMP Companies, Inc.
Fort Worth, TX

Publisher's Cataloging-in-Publication Data
Patterson, T. M. "Roe"

   Crude blessings : the amazing life story of Glenn Patterson,
   American oilman / T. M. "Roe" Patterson. – Fort Worth, TX :
   TMP Companies, Inc., 2018.

   p. ; cm.

   ISBN13: 978-0-9980213-0-0

   1. Patterson, Glenn, 1946- 2. Businessmen—United States—
   Biography. 3. Offshore oil industry—Texas. 4. Petroleum industry
   and trade—Texas. 5. Success in business. I. Title.

HD9570.P37 P37 2018
338.7622338092—dc23   2017919079

Project Coordination by Jenkins Group Inc.
www.bookpublishing.com

Design by Yvonne Fetig Roehler

Printed in the United States of America
22 21 20 19 18 • 5 4 3 2 1

To Tonya, Nathan, and Anna Grace:

Thank you for always loving and supporting me.

This book is also dedicated to

Janeen Patterson, Robert Patterson,

Cloyce and Anita Talbott,

the entire Patterson family,

and all my friends at

Basic Energy Services and Patterson–UTI Energy.

Thank you!

Twenty-five percent of the proceeds from the sale of this book will aid in providing Alzheimer's care, support, and research.

Contents

Foreword

Glenn Patterson's personality and determination built one of the largest oil and gas drilling contractors in North America. His style of leadership created an environment that all companies want and most never achieve. In fact, in my 50-plus years in the industry, I saw it accomplished only twice—Patterson Drilling being the standard bearer.

My first recollection of Glenn Patterson was in the late 1960s. I was managing Snyder Well Servicing Company. Glenn was a college student and would return to Snyder on weekends. He would contact the pusher, wanting to work a couple of days. In a short time, the pushers were contacting him to see whether he would be home over the weekend. Every operator wanted him to work on their crew. He could have treated it casually, like this part-time job didn't matter. But that wasn't Glenn. Everything he did, he put every ounce of himself and his integrity into it.

Glenn graduated college and moved to San Antonio to teach school. Almost immediately, he contacted Snyder Well Service to work summers as a salesman. This was an opportunity to see his uncanny ability to communicate with customers he didn't know. Second to Glenn's work ethic was his ability to communicate, connect, and become close to customers.

I really got to know the true Glenn in 1975, when I married his sister, Anita. Living with her and hearing her stories, it was obvious that Glenn had the characteristics described above since birth. Soon after Anita and I married, in the back of my mind, I wanted to be a partner with Glenn. After much persuasion through 1976 and 1977, he quit teaching school and joined me in forming Patterson Drilling Company.

Neither of us knew anything about the oil and gas drilling business, even though both of us had been around the business most of our lives. Needless to say, things didn't go well. After a couple of years, we had to regroup and rethink our strategy. We started Patterson Drilling in Victoria, Texas. We needed to move the operations to West Texas, where work was a little more plentiful and we could better control our costs. Glenn and his family moved to Snyder at this time.

Working with Glenn on a daily basis, I learned who he was and what he stood for. He was the most honest and caring person I ever met. His word was his bond. He was always for the underdog and always made himself the brunt of the joke. Many times when we would go into a restaurant to eat, our waitress might be an elderly lady who was having a rough time. As we walked out the door, Glenn would give the manager a $100 bill and tell the manager to give it to the waitress after we left.

Glenn never asked anyone to do anything that he wouldn't do personally. He had the cleanest black pickup in the company that he maintained himself for the most part. He expected that all equipment be kept to that standard. He might drop by a clean rig and give a $100 bill to each employee on the crew. No one in the company wanted the wrath of Glenn Patterson when he found equipment that was not to his liking.

There is not enough space or time to tell all of Glenn's stories. The most significant decision we made was to take Patterson public in 1993. After completing the public offering, we were required to take many trips to financial centers all over the United States. Glenn did not like that role and eliminated himself from going on the road by saying, "I am much more valuable staying here and working." When I could get him on the road, Glenn explained operations to Wall Street and did a good job, but he was never comfortable in that environment. Once, when Glenn accompanied me on the road, he was on an escalator in the Waldorf Astoria Hotel in New York City. An elderly lady riding behind him got his attention and said, "Sonny Boy, I don't think you want to go to your meeting with this tag on the sleeve of your suit." Glenn had failed to remove the tags from his new suit. His normal everyday oilfield uniform of blue jeans and boots didn't come with tags to remove. He and I laughed, and he cut the tags off. Not long after that, Glenn made sure I went on these Wall Street trips without him. He looked after operations, and I took care of the "Street." It was an excellent partnership.

The second big decision we made was to merge with UTI in 2001. By this time, we had grown Patterson to 152 rigs. UTI was a similar size, with 151 rigs. Glenn became the president and COO of Patterson-UTI until his failing health in 2005–2006. The larger company enjoyed many profitable years after the merger. We both felt it was one of the best things we could have ever done for our company and shareholders.

This book is a great all-American, feel-good success story. It's also a good read for any CEO who wants to learn how it is possible to survive multiple financial crises, deal with the dangers of bankruptcy, and, in the end, become one of the most financially stable companies in existence. We built a company with strong ethics, integrity, and class that was known for its fairness. This book shows how it is possible for men like Glenn and me to forge these kinds of companies by sticking to these primary principles.

Cloyce Talbott
Former CEO Patterson–UTI Energy, Inc.

Prologue

HARD WORK

It's a day I'll never forget. Saturday morning, early spring. 1986. I was almost 12. Dad shook me awake around 6 a.m.—nothing strange about that. Saturday was a workday; so was Sunday sometimes. He'd been putting us to work on various weekends since elementary school. I worked in the yard, tore down motors, cut up pipe, scrap iron. Hoed weeds, painted. Sandblasted and painted drilling rigs in 100-degree heat or hotter. I did almost everything. My older brother, Robert, had it worse. He actually had to roughneck on the drilling rigs, like a full-grown man. I was still too young for that.

It wasn't easy being the son of a boss—the kid of the legendary founder of Patterson Drilling, Glenn Patterson, who stood 6'4", like LBJ or Abraham Lincoln. He showed no favoritism when it came to work. Quite the opposite, in fact. If there was some rookie job, some shit detail, it was sure to land in your lap. Glenn Patterson had no intention of raising a pair of spoiled brats.

So we piled into the truck without complaining. My dad's best friend from high school, Donnie Newman, was in the truck behind us. It was a long drive through pitch black, leaving the asphalt onto a series of unpaved caliche roads. Dad used the time to think. He was worried. I didn't know all the ins and outs at age 12, but times were bad.

The bottom had fallen out of the oil market. No one was drilling anymore, and Patterson Drilling, the company my father had built from scratch with his brother-in-law, Cloyce Talbott, was flirting with going belly up; they were nearing default on a bank loan. Dad had one last crazy idea to save himself and, thereby, the company—a last-ditch way of drumming up some cash to make an interest-only payment to the bank that he and Cloyce had both resorted to. They had to come up with a few thousand bucks every month. That was our mission that morning as we drove past acres and acres of abandoned oil fields. The price of crude was just too low to keep 'em running—nothing but scrap metal now, which most men would call worthless. But not Glenn Patterson. He saw acres and acres of scrap metal, abandoned flow lines of pipe that no one wanted, and he thought, Even scrap metal has a value. It's something he had learned from his dad. You could cut up metal pipe and repurpose it for fencing and other construction needs. Every oil field has miles and miles of metal pipe used to pump water and oil in and out of the well and transport it throughout the fields. So Dad bought the scrap metal rights from an oil company that had abandoned its lines, and we parked, still in darkness, at one such field. My dad figured that if we could cut a bunch of 2 3/8" pipe into 30-foot lengths and pile it onto the trucks, we might get 50 cents a foot for it. And if eight biceps worked that pipe from dawn to dusk, we could drag away quite a haul. The key was efficiency. Fastest way to cut that pipe was using an acetylene torch, and that was Donnie's job. I had learned how to use a cutting torch, and so had Robert, but Donnie was way faster at it. He would slice through those joints in nine seconds flat. Only problem was that the pipe was red-hot when Donnie dropped it to the ground and moved to the next joint; any nearby brush or grass would instantly catch fire. My job was to rotate the pipe with wrenches as Donnie cut it and to put out these mini fires before they got out of control. I had a shovel and a bucket of sand. So I was running one step behind Donnie as he was slicing through the pipe. Robert and my dad were behind me, grabbing the cut pipe after it cooled and hauling it to the trailers we were towing. The system was working pretty well, but the pipe was not cooling down fast enough. Nearby shrubs kept sprouting up in flame, and I'd have to run back and deal with them. It had been a very dry year, and there was a breeze that morning; the fires started to multiply. I couldn't keep up with them. Pretty soon, one area was out of control and getting worse. I turned to call my dad, but he was already there, assaying the situation—realizing there was little choice. Flames were spreading fast across the dry grass. Glenn ran to the truck and grabbed the radio to report the emergency to the authorities. Then we picked up our gear and parked the trucks upwind. It took a long time for the fire trucks to locate us. We were in the middle of nowhere. Seemed like hours in my panicked 12-year-old mind. The area that was now aflame looked a thousand times larger than the few acres it probably was. It felt like we had torched the whole state of Texas. The day was a bust. I had nightmares about it.

But we're only halfway through the story. It picks up the following Saturday, when Dad woke me up—like clockwork—at 6 a.m. "What are we doin' today?" I asked as we piled into the pickup. "Cutting pipe," he said matter-of-factly. My heart sank. We drove back to that same field—now blackened into a sooty mess—to finish the job. But it went better this time, as Dad knew it would. There was no brush left to slow us down. We got into a rhythm and started stacking those trailers with pipe. It was exhausting work. But no one paused unless Glenn paused—and that happened exactly once in eight hours, just long enough to eat a sandwich. As I wolfed down mine, I started doing the math in my head, something I was pretty good at, even at age 12. We had loaded 150 pieces of the 30-foot pipe lengths before lunch, which my dad was hoping to sell for 50 cents per foot. That was $2,250, plus another $2,250 that afternoon: if we kept up the morning's pace (and didn't start another fire!), $4,500 total.

"How much do you owe the bank?" I asked my dad.

"Millions," said Glenn, not wanting to actually tell me the exact number.

My jaw dropped—I couldn't fathom it. "There's not enough pipe in this whole county! We'll never pay this off with pipe!" I blurted.

"Damn sure won't with that attitude," said Glenn. And we went back to work.

* * *

"Hard work" was not a term that was thrown around lightly in my family. In business today, we associate hard work with success, not necessarily physical work— more the success of a financial or career goal. But there was a time when "hard work" was just that and success was really not part of the conversation. Hard work meant sweat, blood, perseverance, pain, and, finally, a job well done. There was a breed of Americans—the Depression-scarred generation—that believed in hard work, sunup to sundown. They prided themselves on, and almost graded themselves by, how hard they worked, not necessarily by the money they possessed or by their fortunes. Men were measured by their effort first above all things.

My grandfather came from this era. He was a worker of many minor trades: a little farming, a little oil field roughnecking, a little scrap iron recycling, a little whatever he could do to make a buck.

He worked hard at working hard. Never had much to show for it but no one could ever say he wasn't a hard worker. That meant everything to him—everything. My dad was raised by this man and by these principles. Some things get lost generation to generation; my dad took this code with him to his grave. All my dad ever wanted to be known for was hard work. But his story has success too: a multi-billion-dollar company built from scratch—in under three decades. They started Patterson Drilling in 1977 over Thanksgiving turkey and a handshake—my dad and his brother-in-law, Cloyce Talbott—with just a single rig, refurbished from stacked parts.

The oil business has always had its ups and down, with significant fluctuations in supply and demand, but these past four decades have been in a class of their own. We've had almost nonstop war in the Middle East, which precipitated crazy swings in the price for crude. In the mid-'80s crash, many drilling companies went bust; Patterson teetered close to bankruptcy. Twice. But they survived—due in large measure to Cloyce's tenacity, my father's resilience, the culture they fostered, and an undying faith in themselves, each other, and the people around them. It's an example we can all stand to learn from. The company is now part of the S&P 400, worth more than $4 billion at the time I write this.

Most oil field rags-to-riches stories of this ilk come from another era. We think of the oil barons of a bygone time, men who left wakes of destruction in their ascension to wealth and power. Dad was not like that. For men like my father, the hard work ethos also carries with it a code of ethics. It means no lying, no stealing, no backstabbing, no cutting corners. "Fight 'em fair," Glenn would say, and then with a wry grin, he'd jokingly add, "but if that ain't working, try cheatin' a little." But he never cheated. He didn't mind getting the upper hand on a competitor and using it to his advantage, but he wanted to do it fair and square. Business, golf, gin rummy, or ping-pong, he wanted to win, but he wanted to beat you at your best so that you had no excuses. Self-promotion or bragging was a no-no for Glenn. He'd be horrified that I'm writing this book. But someone needed to, and I guess that's on me.

He was honest to a fault and hated a cheater or a liar. He measured people by their heart and their integrity. He was nice to everyone, even his competitors. To Glenn, you deserved kudos when you accomplished much and asked for little recognition or repayment. Dad's code of ethics was built on biblical foundations. I'm not sure he realized until the end of his life that many of his principles were godly, and though he wasn't a very religious man for most of his life, God was working on him and through him all along. Now I'm not saying Glenn was perfect. He wasn't. He had plenty of faults, like we all do, to go along with his finer qualities. But this is a story that tells how God finds you wherever you are, when he's ready, and how, if you're willing, he can work miracles through you.

This is also the story of what happens when success falls squarely in the lap of a hard worker. Something miraculous happens. When the stars align, aspirations are blessed by the Almighty, and things work out perfectly for an outcome that no one could have ever imagined. Some would say that hard work leads to these kinds of fortuitous destinies. Some would say that you have to have some luck to make it.

In his heyday, Dad would say, "I'd rather be lucky than good!"— and then under his breath, he'd say, "Ever notice how lucky a hardworking man can be?" Today he might say, "Ever notice how blessed a good man can be?"

Chapter 1

YOU MAY AS WELL JUST SHOOT ME

As a career oilman, Glenn Patterson took pride in his Patterson company truck more than just about anything. It was shiny and spotless. Always. He had grown up at a time when driving a clean truck said something about the man driving it. Today, we'd say a guy who drives a clean truck is probably a guy who sits at a desk and never goes out into the field much. Not in Glenn's time—you did it all. That's what he expected of his men and of himself. I can remember helping him hose the grime off his truck late one night when I was a kid. He'd been out in the field after hours, visiting a rig that was having some trouble. Several other Patterson employees had driven their trucks to the scene, along with Glenn. I don't recall the specifics of the problem, but it was some kind of blowout that had caused brine water and mud to spew in every direction, covering the roads and drilling location. Dad's truck was a mess when he pulled into our driveway around midnight. I was still up, and Dad put me to work, which I was happy to do. I loved spending time with Dad.

"Let's make this fun," he grinned. "How about we time ourselves?"

That was vintage Dad: make it a contest, find a way to sneak some fun into an otherwise tedious chore. "I'll bet we can get this thing spit shined in four minutes flat."

"Four? How about *three*!" I said cockily. Dad was all in.

"Grab the hose," he said. "Timer starts when the water starts." He glanced at one of the few luxury items he possessed: his Rolex.

"Ready, set … go!" he called out. And the race was on.

I had the hose on full throttle, running around like a maniac, blasting off as much dirt as I could with the maxed-out water pressure. Dad was right there with the sponges and rags. He was getting completely drenched, grinning from ear to ear. The Rolex was waterproof. With one minute to go, I turned off the hose and grabbed the shammy to get the windows, while Dad dried the hood with our old towels. We were a great team.

OK, so there were a few streaks here and there and a droplet or two of water when the clock finally stopped. But the job was basically done. Dad put his arm around me and nodded in satisfaction. He had made his point. Several points, actually.

To me, he was saying: anything can be fun. It's all in your attitude.

To his employees (the guys who had driven home the previous night with trucks just as messy as Glenn's), he was leading by example. He was saying: no matter how late it is or how tired you are, company property gets treated with care and respect. There's no way he was going to drive into the Patterson yard the next day with anything but a spotless truck. The other guys knew it, and you better believe they were out there on their driveways just like Glenn, getting the last speck buffed out before going to bed that night or first thing in the morning. Dad would've had trouble sleeping if he hadn't taken care of the dirt on his truck before bed. That's just the way he rolled.

And there was nothing quite like being out on the open road for my father in his spit-shined company truck. Wind in his hair, smooth ride, gazing at the horizon. It's where he did his best thinking: barreling down the interstate, one arm on the wheel, the other with the phone or resting on the open window. He liked to feel the breeze, even when it was hot.

He drove way too fast and got several speeding tickets over the years. When my mother was in the truck, he'd stack mail in front of the speedometer so Mom couldn't see how fast he was going. But if my brother or I ever happened to get a speeding ticket, well, that was another story: we'd be on the receiving end of an hour-long ass chewing.

Dad drove the same basic ride his entire life, a half-ton truck with an extended cab. It was the pickup that the "tool pushers" drove—the rig managers who worked for him. Glenn was not big on hierarchy, though he was the only guy who got a *black* truck. That didn't bother the guys; black was a pain, they'd say. Too hard to keep clean—especially if you worked for Glenn Patterson. Everything at Patterson was a team effort. It didn't matter if you were the boss or the janitor. That's why he drove his half-ton Chevy with the extended cab: he didn't want to stick out. It was about camaraderie. We're in this together—one team, through the good seasons and the bad. It motivated people to do their best. Everyone worked hard at Patterson, none more so than Glenn—and clients loved that. He'd be covered in grease like the rest of them.

And he played cards with the guys after hours. Gin rummy or Booray. It was usually gin and always for money; flop gin, they called it. Nothing too crazy. He played gin with Cloyce more than anyone. The stakes of those games were a little higher. But money rarely changed hands; the running total was tallied in a pocket notebook that Cloyce kept. Once in a while, especially after some really great news, they'd settle the tab.

It was a blood sport for my father. Playing cards brought out Glenn's competitive streak. Not that he had to win; it's that Glenn refused to lose. If someone dared say "rummy," the first words out of Glenn's mouth would be: "You win … How 'bout double or nothin'?" Which meant it could go on for hours. But beware if you drove into the yard on a late Sunday afternoon to play cards in a messy truck. Glenn was obsessive about neatness. Shops, pickups, drilling rigs, yards, even my room!

There was this often-repeated story around Patterson about the time when one of Glenn's hands drove into the yard with a pickup covered in mud. The hapless guy walked inside where everyone was playing cards. He may have been late, too, which was another one of Dad's pet peeves: an obsession with punctuality—which meant 15 minutes early. So this guy was both late and messy.

The game stopped; Glenn had lost his concentration. He could see the dirty truck through the window, and it was driving him crazy. He stood up suddenly from the card table and marched outside. Rolling up his sleeves, Glenn grabbed some rags and a hose and started washing the poor bastard's truck. The tool pusher finally noticed: "What the hell?" Dad had moved his truck closer to the wash rack to hose it down. A couple of older managers said, "I'd get out there and help if I were you." The sheepish tool pusher darted outside to give Glenn a hand. They washed the truck in silence together. Not a word was spoken.

The incident taught everyone at Patterson a lesson they never forgot. Dad did that often, grabbed a push broom if the shop was dirty, picked up a rig brush if a rig was in need of attention, or swept out a field office with everyone watching. They never watched for long. They were cleaning beside him in no time, and no one said much. Message delivered loud and clear: "Take pride in all you do for Patterson Drilling. I better not find this dirty again."

It was this work ethic that had paved the way for Glenn's success. And that success was the stuff of legend, which is what made June 10, 2010, so painful and poignant. It's the day we had to take away the one thing my father still took a great deal of pride in: his truck.

He was not quite 64 at the time, but the Lewy body dementia and Alzheimer's, which had started five years earlier, were deteriorating to the point of making him a hazard behind the wheel, to himself and to others in Snyder, Texas—population: 10,000. It's a small town. Everyone knew it. Except Glenn Patterson. That's why my mother, Janeen, had asked me to show up along with my older brother, Robert. We needed a family intervention.

People had been complaining about Glenn's driving for months. He'd been cutting people off, driving all over the road, and pulling out in front of folks. More than once the local sheriff would go over to the house to pay him a visit. He'd say, "Mr. Patterson, you know you gotta be a little more careful out there." The sheriff would have his hat off, holding it in his hands, very deferential. This was Glenn Patterson, after all—town patriarch and once its biggest employer. My mother, Janeen, would be pouring the coffee, treading gingerly, knowing what she knew about Glenn's temper. It didn't happen often, but when that Patterson smokestack blew, it was epic. The first telltale warning sign was the little white bead of saliva that would form in one corner of Glenn's mouth. Janeen and Glenn had been together for forty years. She knew it was coming.

"Whoever's doin' the complaining, well, they oughta come around and look me in the eye, don't you think?" Glenn slammed down his coffee and rose to his feet to make his point. Glenn was a hard man to say no to when he stood towering over you. "Don't I have a right to face my accuser? Last I checked we were still in America."

"Well, you see, Mr. Patterson," stammered the well-meaning sheriff, "the thing is, well, there are *multiple* complaints ..."

"Multiple?" Glenn raised his eyebrows. "How many's it got to be to qualify as '*multiple*'? Two? Three?" Glenn was not really asking. "How about those three complainers do the neighborly thing of getting their asses over here for a one-on-one conversation? Don't you think that's fair, Sheriff?"

And on it went. What could the poor lawman do? There was no arguing with Glenn Patterson at full tilt. It happened a few times— more complaints, more visits by the law. I even had a couple of phone calls with the sheriff to try to coach him on how to approach my dad, but it never worked. He always left without taking away Glenn's license.

I was working for Basic Energy, at the time, in Midland, Texas, an hour or so drive from Snyder, where we'd grown up. So I wasn't around for those daily battles and the increasing impairment my mom was seeing in Dad, including the loss of memory and motor function. None of us could handle it, to tell the truth. The man who would not stop was being forced, finally, to stop—placed under de facto "house arrest" by his own family. It would devastate him, we knew. It would take all of us being present: myself, Robert, my mother, and Cloyce, Glenn's brother-in-law and business partner of three decades. Robert and I had asked that Cloyce be a part of it. We didn't quite know how to approach the situation. Dad was so intimidating, so larger-than-life. It would be like going in and telling Ronald Reagan, "You're not gonna drive anymore." He might listen to Cloyce over us.

I arrived late. They had already started the discussion. Dad had tears in his eyes, which was a very strange thing for me to witness. I had never seen my father cry. Not once. I wondered whether it was a symptom of Alzheimer's, as I sat down and said, "What's going on, Dad?"

"Not a damn thing good," responded Glenn. He was hopping mad. My brother, I saw, was teary-eyed—Mom, also; she quietly left the room.

"We're trying to talk your daddy into not driving," said Cloyce matter-of-factly.

"Well, that's something we sure need to talk about," I said.

Dad's eyes bored into me: "You're the one? The guy who's taking *my* pickup?" The spittle had started to form in the corner of Glenn's mouth.

"Why don't we just hire a driver?" Cloyce offered. "If we need to go somewhere, let's just get us a driver. I'll use him, too."

Cloyce had no use for a driver; he was trying to smooth the argument.

"Dad, that's a good idea," I chimed in.

"I can't figure out why everybody's ganging up on me," he exploded. "Why don't y'all just kill me?"

"Come on, Dad," I protested, "it's not that bad. This is just one of those things. You're gonna hurt somebody; you're gonna hurt yourself …"

"Just kill me. Y'all just take me outside and shoot me. That'd be better. If I can't drive anymore, that's what I want," he declared. "I want to be dead."

"Calm down, Dad," Robert said and tried to put a hand on his shoulder, but Dad brushed it aside.

"I'm not good for anything anymore," he brooded. "Just take me out and shoot me. I'm not gonna be a burden to y'all."

"You're not a burden," Robert insisted. "We love you; that's why we're doing this." I echoed Robert's comment. It did not help.

The biggest problem was that Glenn didn't think he had a problem. That's the saddest part about Alzheimer's: the denial.

He had this thing in his mind that he wasn't sick—even though he was getting lost in his own house, even though he'd wander off and forget his way home. He'd been getting paranoid about things he saw on TV, imagining prowlers in the house, killers. A conspiracy. That's what this intervention felt like to him: people out to get him. It broke my heart.

In rare moments of lucidity, he'd realize the truth about his condition. But then he'd forget all about it the next day. "Don't you remember, Dad?" I'd say. "You've been diagnosed with Alzheimer's …"

"Well, that's not true," he'd insist. "Don't know who told you that, but there's not a damn bit of truth to it."

And so it went. This happens to millions of families, I'm sure. The disease is just devastating; you never know what you're going to get at any given moment. The worst moment by far for us had been two years earlier, when his peers were honoring Dad in a very public event, where he'd be expected to address the crowd and give an acceptance speech.

It was January 24, 2008, the Top Hand banquet of the Permian Basin Petroleum Association, one of those rare occasions where Glenn had to lose the jeans and put on a suit and tie—he kept the boots, though. Glenn's boots were always spit-shined like his car. You took care of your belongings.

Both Glenn and Cloyce were being given what amounted to a lifetime achievement award at that evening's banquet, which took place at the Petroleum Club in Midland, a 90-minute drive from Snyder. Everyone in the family was concerned about whether Glenn would be able to pull off his acceptance speech. First of all, there was the matter of the long car ride. Robert and I were nervous as hell as we waited for Cloyce, Anita (Cloyce's wife, Dad's sister), Mom, and Dad to arrive. I was checking my cell phone every

10 seconds for calamitous news. But they pulled up right on schedule; Glenn handed the keys to the valet and gave me a look: What's everyone so freaked out about? Robert and I exchanged expressions of relief: maybe he'll be able to pull this off without a hitch, after all.

But as the banquet got under way, a stream of well-wishers paraded past the honorees' table. Colleagues and friends slapped Glenn on the back and offered him their congratulations. Dad did well, but he started to get disoriented. I could see it in his eyes. He didn't recognize these people—folks he had known for years. I glanced at my wife, Tonya. She squeezed my hand under the table; she knew I was anxious.

No one but close family knew about Glenn's Alzheimer's diagnosis, largely because of his own denial. They knew he was behaving differently but not the full extent of his condition. I wondered what was going to happen when he got called to the podium.

What was meant to be a career-crowning moment could easily turn into an ignominious and very public humiliation. I made eye contact with my mom, sitting next to Dad across the banquet table. She looked serene, not at all worried. It's in the Lord's hands, she seemed to say.

My mother believed that everything happened for a reason; her faith runs deep. She needed it, given all the ups and downs in her life. She had practiced Dad's remarks with him over and over, and now she had turned it over to God. Sadly, my own faith was eluding me that particular evening. Worried as heck, I felt my heart pound as the announcer stood up to present the awards.

"Operating on faith and living on a shoestring, Glenn Patterson and Cloyce Talbott combined their skills and knowledge of drilling, rigs, and business in the late 1970s to form Patterson Drilling," said Tom Kelly, a customer and a close friend of Dad's, who was the emcee for the evening. He did a great job setting the stage: "In the first two years, they lost $800,000 and four of their seven partners.

"Today, the company's known as Patterson-UTI Energy and, with a market cap over $4 billion, ranks as the second-largest drilling contractor in the United States. It actually takes the number one spot if you go by total number of feet drilled." There were whistles and cheers; colleagues shouted out, "Go, Glenn!" His eyes darted around the room—What the heck's going on around here?

Uh-oh, I thought. Tonya squeezed my hand.

They summoned Glenn to the stage when it was his turn to speak. He stood up just fine, but as he made his way toward the podium, cell phones came out, bulbs flashing. Glenn blinked in disorientation; the crowd roared, he squinted, blinked, teetered slightly ...

I closed my eyes. And prayed.

Chapter 2

HIS HANDS WERE AS HARD AS HIS HEAD

"Dirt-poor" was how my father described his upbringing. They had very little but always just barely enough to eke out a living. A century gone by in the great state of Texas, which was still, to some extent, frontier land back then, a place where men became men the hard way: with blistered lips and whiskey. Slinging guns, watching their backs, and never giving up.

My grandfather, Monroe Patterson, was one of them. Known as "Scrap Iron" most of his days for his affinity to cut up and recycle bulk metals—that, or he was just tougher than iron. I called him Papaw or Paw-Paw like all the other grandkids. I remember being fascinated by his hands. The sheer size was impressive; then there was the coarse texture of his weathered skin. Pick any finger, I thought, and you could light a match. He was a chain-smoker. I liked to watch him pull out his trusty pouch of Prince Albert tobacco and roll his cigarettes. Paw-Paw didn't talk much. Rarely opened his mouth, in fact, unless it was to smoke. When he did speak to me, I listened closely; I was not the best kid, but I straightened up around Dad or Monroe. Dad also said Monroe could drink hard from time to time. I never saw that side.

His wife, Eudell Patterson, was a rock of a woman. She had to be to put up with Monroe. It takes a strong woman to love a man like that and raise his kids. Didn't hurt that she stood 6 feet tall. My father was third in line, after two older sisters, Charlene and Anita. Then came another boy, Alton, which was good news, as far as Monroe was concerned. Not that he minded the girls. It was a practical thing: boys had stronger arms, and he planned to put those biceps to use.

Glenn came into the world in 1946, in the very first wave of the baby boomers, nine months give or take after the GIs came home from Europe and the Pacific. He was born on the same ranch where his mother was born in Blackwell, Texas, population: 320—about as far from glamorous as you can get. Things may have been hopping in 1946 if you lived on the coasts: industries humming, manufacturing taking off, plenty of jobs, and plenty of money in circulation. Not so much in Blackwell. It felt more like a lingering version of the Great Depression.

Blackwell's name had nothing to do with oil. It had been Jamestown originally, but the town elders changed the name in 1906 to Blackwell, after one of the railroad's major stockholders, Henry Blackwell. They figured it was the only way for a Podunk town to get noticed, and the ruse worked; they literally put themselves on the map when the railroad announced that its westbound line to New Mexico would be routed through the tiny town of Blackwell, which immediately erected a post office and became a shipping hub for three nearby counties. It didn't achieve as much as the elders had hoped, however. The population doubled for a decade or two, then fell back to its baseline of 300. Not an easy place to make a living.

My grandmother's family owned a little orchard and a small farm in Blackwell, which put something on the family table. Peaches mainly, not much money. They were barely eking by. Monroe took a good look at the business prospects in Blackwell and decided he needed a bigger pond to make it like he hoped to, so he carted his family to Anton, outside of Lubbock, to work on a dairy farm. He still wasn't making the kind of living he wanted, and the dairy work eventually dried up, so he headed for the Snyder area. Even with its modest population of 10,000, Snyder was still 30 times larger than Blackwell. And being closer to Midland, which stands at the heart of the Permian Basin—one of the most prolific oil- and gas-producing regions in the country—it afforded more opportunity for work. And that's exactly what Monroe did, sunup to sundown. He did it all. Scrap metal business, roughnecking in the oil patch, whatever it took. Monroe also ran a "rat hole" operation, meaning a truck-mounted drilling rig that comes into an oil field early before the main drilling rig. Two holes are drilled; we call them a "rat hole" and a "mouse hole," around 20–25 feet deep. These holes are where you store drill pipe during the main drilling operation, when the main drilling rig makes connections in and out of the oil well being drilled. The "rat hole" team also starts the first pilot hole for the actual oil well. It's backbreaking work in rough terrain and blistering heat. On a good job, my grandfather might have two or three hands with him, and he worked them to the bone. Sometimes it was just Monroe and one other guy.

Eudell's brothers were also tool pushers, running larger drilling rigs for various companies. So family fortunes swayed up and down with the price of crude. Monroe's motto remained the same no matter what: I'll outhustle the next guy. That's the way he operated, the legacy he left to his kids.

Glenn was young when he joined the crew. He learned about hard work the hard way … before he even learned much at school. Dad was smart; he just wasn't the kind of smart that fits in a box. He didn't learn much from books. He would learn from people, from situations. He could be anywhere, facing anyone, and know just what to say. It's an intelligence and an instinct that came from his gut. Public school bored him. The system wasn't designed for guys like Glenn, who thrive in situations that are practical and hands-on, rather than abstract book learning. Donnie Newman was exactly the same way, which is why he and Glenn bonded for life in their disdain of the West Texas school system, playing hooky as often as possible and getting into brawls.

Dad was very small for his age entering high school, so he knew what it was like to be the little guy whom people picked on. By the time he was a senior, he had grown quite a bit, while Donnie was just the opposite: short and stocky but still strong as an ox. Dad and Donnie looked like Mutt and Jeff. They were quite the duo, developing a reputation—like a pair of superheroes—for sticking up for the underdog. As Snyder High upperclassmen, their brawls and serial truancy became legendary. They'd skip school and go to the pool hall or the racetrack in Abilene, with a case of beer on ice in the trunk, which was surprisingly easy to get. They'd drive across the tracks to the black neighborhood on the east side of town, where the police either turned a blind eye or were too shorthanded to control it, and you could buy beer at practically any age. Donnie and Glenn did pretty much as they pleased.

In Glenn's senior year, he didn't open his school locker. Not once. He'd forgotten where it was located, in fact, so he had to go into the office on the last day of school to ask for his locker number so he could retrieve and return the books he never once opened. But he graduated somehow.

After high school, Snyder didn't have much to offer. Monroe kept his "rat hole" operation as busy as he could, and Glenn was often part of the crew. While nothing fancy, it was a living wage. But Glenn had an epiphany at age 20, when he looked around the

oil field one day at the unshaven, bourbon-gargling, blistered, sun-
burned, and lonely men, and he thought, "I gotta get the hell out of
here." (He'd be back!)

He started attending some college classes, inspired, in part, by
his sisters and my mother, whom he had started to date. They were
taking classes at San Angelo State, about a hundred miles south
of Snyder. Dad's approach to college wasn't much different from
the one he had in high school. He seemed to pass classes without
much effort while working the oil patch on weekends and nonclass
hours to pay for school. His goal was to get the degree. My mother,
Janeen, was different. She was passionate about learning and worked
hard at her studies.

Janeen had a dream, a vision for her life. Her family owned both
of the movie theaters in town, so she grew up watching Hollywood
films. Janeen had become enamored of actors and acting and wanted
to make movies her life. But she also was practical about it; she
had assistant directed a few of the high school plays and enjoyed
working with other students. So, instead of struggling to make it as
an actress, she decided: Why not teach instead? Her plan was to go
to college to get her teaching certificate to teach high school drama.
And Glenn thought, "I could do that. I could teach. Anything but
the oil field."

Glenn had met Janeen through Donnie, who was dating her
best friend at the time. They had wanted Glenn and Janeen to hook
up so they'd be a foursome. But it didn't happen right away. Janeen
thought, initially, that Glenn was a little too wild for her. Not that
she didn't have her own wild side. She already had a kid by then and
had been married. Twice. Both guys, by coincidence, were named
Bill.

In high school, Janeen had fallen for Bill Watkins, a roughneck
who liked his liquor. There was something dangerously attractive

about Bill. It happens when we're young: we're often drawn to the very things that hurt us. The worse Bill seemed to treat Janeen, the more she tried. They weren't married long before she was pregnant and stuck in a marriage that wasn't working. Bill's drinking got worse, and he once became abusive. That day, she quietly packed her bags and left for good.

Janeen did not want to raise her newborn on her own, however. There was another guy named Bill, entirely different in character. A teetotaler, in fact. Bill Haun was older, a kind former marine who worked as a highway patrolman. Haun had a protective streak. He wanted to take care of Janeen and Robert, which was irresistible for Janeen, who accepted his proposal of marriage. But even this one would end badly. Tragically, in fact.

Officer Haun was driving his patrol car one afternoon in 1968, with little Robert, almost two at the time, sitting next to him in the front seat. This was long before the era of infant car seats—we barely wore seat belts back then. Bill had been having some trouble with the accelerator in his patrol car; it had a habit of getting stuck at the most inopportune moments. But it hadn't happened for a while, so he wasn't particularly worried that afternoon. When the car started accelerating wildly as they crossed a narrow bridge over a creek in San Antonio, Bill panicked. He jammed on the brakes, but they didn't work—or, in his confusion, he may have been pressing the accelerator by mistake, making matters even worse.

The car went skidding off the narrow bridge and plunged into the creek. By a miracle, my brother, Robert, was not injured by the impact, but Officer Haun could not move and he was bleeding badly. The wheel-mounted gearshift had impaled him in the gut. The car was completely submerged, filling rapidly with water.

By God's grace, someone happened to be nearby—a man on horseback, who dismounted and dived headlong into the creek to help. He swam around to the driver's side at first, but Officer Haun motioned frantically toward Robert next to him, barely visible through the glass and water. The horseman swam around and forced open the passenger door, pulling the toddler to safety. The patrolman was not so lucky. He died, and Mom was a single mother again.

A heartbroken Janeen moved back in with her parents for a second time. After several months of grieving and constant prodding by friends, she started dating Glenn, who seemed to have the right balance of wild and dependable. Janeen was a good influence on Glenn. She showed him that you didn't have to be a victim of your circumstances. That, despite setbacks, you could still have a vision for your life. Janeen's dream involved going to college. Why not? thought Glenn.

Both of his sisters, Charlene and Anita, had gone to college to learn practical business skills that offered a less menial line of work. Glenn decided that's what he wanted to do: study business. Or something. Anything to get away from the oil field. But the Pattersons, unlike Janeen's family, had not one iota of disposable income. If Glenn wanted to go to college, he'd have to pay his own way. So Glenn kept one foot in the oil field, working long hours on weekends to cover his tuition.

It must have been grueling. The commute from college to his oil field jobs sometimes clocked in at two hours in each direction. He'd be going nonstop, barely enough time to study, covered in grease. I can't imagine the number of times my father must have scrubbed his blistered hands to show up for class at San Angelo State and hold my mother's books. Or take *her* hand. As she felt Glenn's coarse skin, she must have thought what I thought about Paw-Paw: pick any finger and you could light a match.

Chapter 3

A CRUEL
DAMN DISEASE

That awful afternoon in early June 2010—when I drove away from Dad's house after taking away his truck keys, along with his sense of liberty—was easily the hardest in my life, His, too, I'm sure. But what followed got even worse. He wasn't joking about wanting to be dead. Robert hadn't wanted to leave him alone after I drove off that day. Cloyce had left, too, and Mom was running an errand, so it was just the two of them in the house: Robert and Glenn.

"I'm done," said Glenn. "I'm just done." There was nothing petulant about it. It was fatalistic. "I need to be dead." That was his simple conclusion.

Then he'd spin to Robert and say: "Why don't you leave?"

"Y'all need to go," he'd persist. "Go on home." But Robert refused to depart. He thought Glenn was going to grab his gun and do something stupid. He didn't leave until Mom got back and things settled down.

Two weeks later, Robert's suspicions were confirmed when I showed up at the house and realized that Dad had been messing around with his 9-mm automatic. He was trying unsuccessfully to cock it. It's the one time that I actually thanked God for the Alzheimer's—his compromised motor control and confusion around planning made it impossible to chamber a round.

"Take a look at this damn thing," he growled. "I think it's broken."

"What are you planning to do with it?" I inquired apprehensively.

"Just want to load it, make sure it works," Glenn responded.

"Why?" I persisted.

"I just do!" barked my father. "What if someone was breakin' in here?"

But I suspected he had another motive, and my heart sank. The man who *never* quit—who never gave in to adversity, always pushed ahead no matter what, and modeled that for everyone around him—was ready to quit. Or so I thought, anyway. I tried to get inside his head. As terrible as Alzheimer's and Lewy body dementia are for family members, we can only imagine how bad they must be for the person actually suffering from the afflictions. My dad must have felt powerless, which was a horrible feeling for him.

Maintaining control of his own destiny, that was paramount to Glenn Patterson. Calamities and rough waters aside, a man had to feel like he was steering the ship—at least, he needed that illusion.

"You gonna help me with this or not?" He pointed to the gun. It was devastating.

We went back and forth a few times. I knew I had to grab that weapon and get the hell out of there. But I didn't want to upset my father even more. So I created an elaborate distraction involving food and television to get my father's mind on something other than the gun. It worked, thank God. Pretty soon he was engrossed in something on TV, a crime show. But that was its own kind of curse; Glenn believed sometimes that what he was seeing was real. He'd be horrified by all the murder and mayhem on every channel. "You see that?" He'd point frantically to the screen. "My God! That's horrible. How could they let it happen?"

I managed to sneak the 9 mm into my mother's open safe and locked it. I knew Dad could no longer get into it, either. I told Mom what had happened, and she was not surprised. "He asked the same of me. I just changed the subject," she said. She was glad I had hidden the gun, and she was eager to change the subject herself. But I drove away in tears.

It had been *years* of tears at that point. I remember several winters back when we asked Dad to sign some papers. It was becoming increasingly necessary for Glenn to relinquish control of business matters, but he fought us like the devil each time. We had managed somehow to persuade him on this occasion to comply with the lawyer's and accountant's advice, but when it came time to put his signature on the document, he just didn't know where to begin. I stared at him; others were chatting across the room, not paying attention to Glenn, who was entirely confused by the pen and paper that sat before him on the desk. They were like alien objects. He squinted, trying to make sense of the situation. It felt like minutes. Then he picked up the pen. More squinting—What am I supposed to do with this thing? I decided not to come to his rescue this time. I wanted to see how bad it had gotten.

Glenn finally figured out he was supposed to be signing at the *X*, but the last indignity was that he had forgotten his own signature. Glenn ended up chicken-scratching a few scribbles, like a toddler. He practiced on a newspaper for about 10 minutes. He finally got it to his satisfaction and signed the document. The signature was poor, but it was good enough for Dad, and he was excited that he had finally signed the paper. I could tell he felt human for a brief moment. It's a cruel damn disease.

People have remarked how Alzheimer's puts people back where they started. But that's a pretty romanticized view in my book. It's the dead opposite of the wonder of infancy, where each discovery is a little miracle. Alzheimer's combined with Lewy body dementia is more of a nightmare—at least for Glenn it was.

Glenn had a close friend named Rusty Melton. When Dad could no longer drive, Rusty would come by and get him out of the house. Rusty and Glenn went back all the way to their teens in Snyder. They had become business partners in the early '80s when Dad helped Rusty start an oil field dirt construction company called Melco. Glenn had done this multiple times during his career: helping people start businesses, loaning money or equipment for various ventures. As long as he believed in the individual, Glenn would do just about anything to help someone get a leg up or start a business or dig their way out of some kind of mess.

As Rusty and Glenn were close friends over the years, Rusty was happy to help out when Glenn could no longer drive. Dad was comfortable with Rusty coming to drive him because it felt more like two friends just out for coffee or breakfast. Maybe a drive out to Glenn's ranch to look around. But it never felt like a caregiver taking Dad away from the house to give my mother a break. But that's truly what it was. Until it got too much for Rusty to handle. Dad got to where just going to the restroom became confusing, and that's when Rusty could no longer handle the excursions.

When Dad lost control of his body, it became too much for my mom to take care of him at home too. In anticipation of this moment, we had already found an assisted-living facility with a dementia/Alzheimer's/memory care ward called Raider Ranch in

Lubbock, which was 90 miles away, a bit of a haul. But we had scouted every facility in the area, and this, we felt sure, was the best. The problem was how to get him there without a scene or causing him to be upset. It would involve a long car ride, which Glenn was beginning to find less and less tolerable. It was four of us in the car: myself at the wheel, Dad in the passenger seat, and our two wives in back. We thought it would comfort him to have all of us along for the ride, but it only made him suspicious.

"Where the hell you taking me?" he demanded.

"We're just going to Lubbock to see your doctor," I lied. We'd agreed, for now, to keep it vague.

"The hell we are," he yelled. "You're trying to get rid of me!"

He meant it literally. "I know where we're going!" he repeated over and over.

He had no idea where we were going, of course, but having me driving the car, and Mom in the back seat, was different enough from his regular day-to-day. At that time, anything different for Dad was bad. He was paranoid and disoriented. He thought we were driving him out into the desert to shoot him.

He kept looking forward through the windshield and freaking out: the oncoming asphalt, poles whizzing by, cars in other lanes. It was too much for him, too much sensory information all at once. I was trying to keep it as steady as I could, but Dad couldn't bear it. The ride was so overwhelming for him that every so often, he'd lurch over and try to grab at the wheel. I'd have to fend him off or go skidding across lanes. It was treacherous. Everyone had tears in their eyes. My normally thick-skinned mother was bawling at times.

"Glenn, you're scaring me!" she told him.

That would settle him a little, but it wouldn't last long. A few minutes later, he'd look at me and look out the window and get upset again. By the time we got to Raider Ranch, everyone was a wreck. I had been texting Robert about the drive. Yep, while on the freeway with my passenger freaking out and grabbing at the wheel—to add even more jeopardy to an already dangerous situation. Robert was already there, waiting for us at Raider Ranch. I had to let him know what to expect, to be ready for all hell to break loose when we got there. But to everyone's surprise, Glenn seemed to calm down at Raider Ranch. He ate, and we talked and laughed, and he started to relax.

My mother later told me that final hour in the car with Dad was the most challenging moment of her life. That's really saying something, given everything that Mom had been through. But I know exactly what she meant. I had just set a new world record of my own for the hardest drive of my life.

Chapter 4

GOODBYE TO THE OIL FIELD

It's a mythic place, the oil field. Not a particular field, per se. More like *all* the oil fields merged into one. That's the "oil field" that Glenn left behind when he finally got his degree from San Angelo State. Donnie, meanwhile, had been shipped off to Vietnam along with another friend of theirs, Robert Sterling. They'd never be the same.

Glenn had been drafted, too; Janeen was just crushed when he received his draft notice. She was in no mood to lose *another* man. My mother prayed for a miracle—and she got one.

It was during the physical exam. Glenn had stripped down to his briefs to go through an inspection line, where everyone was weighed, measured, and asked a series of routine medical questions by a doctor who, the story goes, was chain-smoking cigarettes! It was a stressful job, to be sure, sending all of these young boys off to war. There were a surprising number of easily treatable medical conditions that would get you a waiver from service, such as gastritis, ulcers, hepatitis, and anemia. They had psychological disqualifiers, too, and everyone, in 1969, was gaming the system to get a rejection. People would stay awake for four days straight before their exam.

Ted Nugent, apparently, didn't bathe for a month, used meth, and acted like a homeless bum.

Not Dad. Even though he had ambivalence about the war in Vietnam, Glenn felt duty bound to serve his country. He showed up willingly without excuses. But the chain-smoking medic saw something in Glenn's innocent face that gave him pause. Who knows exactly what he saw: his earnest eyes, a sense of promise, perhaps? The doctor just sighed and wrote "hernia" on Glenn's card—an automatic disqualifier. Glenn drove away in a state of uncertainty, not elated but not unhappy either. Dad felt perfectly fine, and he had told the medic as much. But the doctor was playing God that afternoon; he decided on a whim to spare Glenn Patterson from combat service in Southeast Asia. When Glenn told Janeen, she glanced up to the clouds and thanked God. Glenn never did have an issue with the "hernia."

They went on to graduate college in 1972; Janeen was offered a job right away, teaching drama at a school in San Antonio. She asked Glenn to drive her down to check it out one day. It was a sunny morning in August, blazing hot, when they hopped into Janeen's Cutlass Oldsmobile; her dad had bought it for her as a graduation present. Glenn took the wheel, and they headed south, smiles on their faces and wind in their hair.

Somewhere along that three-hour ride, Glenn gazed pensively at the southern horizon and saw his future. San Angelo, where they'd gone to school, was already 100 miles south of Snyder, and San Antonio was 200 miles farther. Glenn was leaving the oil-rich Permian Basin—both literally and metaphorically. And it felt good.

If my sweetheart is moving to San Antonio, thought Glenn, well, hell, that's where I'm moving, too! I could teach as well, he reasoned. That way they'd be together.

In fact …

"Look, there's a red bucket on the side of the road right there," Glenn said, pointing out the window. "It says 'Justice of the Peace.'"

His eyes widened. "Hey, let's get married right there."

That was his wedding proposal.

Janeen's eyes widened even more than Glenn's. She knew this day was coming; it had been almost four years in the making— practically an eternity for my mom, who had been married twice before she even turned 20. Now she was 24, feeling both giddy and flustered at the same time as they pulled over to get married by a justice of the peace.

"What makes you think this'll work?" she hemmed. "How'd you know they perform weddings here?"

"Let's find out," said Glenn, marching inside. Janeen scurried to catch up, but before she even reached the front door, Glenn reemerged with a thumbs-up. "All good," he smiled. "We'll come back next week." And that was that.

He opened the car door for my mom, whose mind was still spinning. It was vintage Glenn: a spontaneous decision … with a specific timetable. Janeen had thought for a moment that they were going to do it right then and there. But Dad wanted to come back looking more put together, with proper rings.

It remains one of my brother, Robert's, most vivid and earliest memories. He was only five at the time, when, one week later, Dad showed up at our grandparents' house dressed in a bright purple suit. It was something festive that he had grabbed from a thrift store. "Why are you all dressed up like that?" asked Robert. He was eating Cheerios at the breakfast table. "Your mother and I are getting married," grinned Glenn.

In came Janeen, wearing her best dress. She stared at Glenn in his hideous maroon suit and laughed. They drove down Route 83 to the justice of the peace they'd found one week prior. Glenn had procured their marriage license in San Angelo a few days earlier. The aging justice squinted at it. Nodded.

"Well," he glanced at the couple, "shall we get this show on the road?"

"Yes sir," answered Glenn, squeezing Janeen's hand.

The justice had the TV on with a baseball game going on in the background as he performed the ceremony. He got to the line "if anyone gathered here has reason to object to this union" then paused and said, "Guess we can skip that part." There was no one in the room but the three of them.

Before allowing the newlyweds to kiss, however, the justice looked Glenn in the eye and said: "Now, son, I've never performed a wedding ceremony where there was a divorce—and I don't expect this one to turn out like that." Glenn assured him, "Oh, no sir, no sir." (True to his word, they were married 43 years.)

Glenn also kept his word to find a job in San Antonio—teaching like Janeen, but at a different school on the other side of town. Janeen taught drama at McCullough High School in the Southside District, and Glenn taught at Marshall High in the north, commuting every day in the Oldsmobile. He was an instructor for the local chapter of DECA, the Distributive Education Clubs of America, which provided vocational and life skills training to kids who didn't quite fit into traditional schooling. In other words, kids like Glenn.

He'd teach them how to open a bank account and balance their checkbooks, how to change the oil in their car, how to type a résumé, how to apply for a job—practical, actionable knowledge for blue-collar kids. The DECA program even allowed these teenagers to go to school for the first half of the day, then go to work for the other half. It was deeply satisfying for Dad, the sort of program he wished he could've had when he was skipping school in Snyder. Glenn was, by all accounts, an inspired teacher. The kids loved him. He was a natural. The teachers loved him, too; not only was Glenn affable but also he was handy. He used to fix their cars on the weekend to make a few extra dollars.

Glenn remained friends for life with this group of teachers and especially the school principal, John Kloza, even when he was running a billion-dollar drilling company. Years later, after he bought the family farm in Blackwell, where he was born, he'd invite the San Antonio teachers over for a weekend of hunting.

On one particular trip in the late '80s, I remember they started playing cards, eating and drinking on Friday afternoon, and they never quit until late Sunday when they all had to go home. No one ever loaded a gun or fired a shot. The deer were safe. All they wanted to do was catch up and have fun. Dad had me go out the following week to hunt a doe, which he butchered and shipped to the teachers. He felt bad about the fact that they'd gone home empty-handed. Dad really enjoyed the camaraderie during those years at Marshall High School, though he wished he had been earning more.

Mom, on the rougher south side of San Antonio, was having a tougher time of it. There were some troubled kids in her acting class, one of whom had it in for her. Things got trickier when I came into the picture in 1974, when they had a newborn and a seven-year-old in the same house—a tiny house they were renting but could ill afford on two public school teacher salaries. They were still using Mom's bedroom suite from back home, sharing her old full-sized bed, which was designed for a kid, not two full-grown adults, one of whom was 6'4". Dad's feet dangled off the edge of the bed like that Dr. Seuss character named Ned from *One Fish, Two Fish*. Mom, who was feeling pretty cramped herself, decided it was time for a new bedroom suite, something my father knew they could not afford. So he came up with a classic Glenn Patterson plan: using the meager savings they had, they'd take a one-night vacation to Las Vegas, where they'd "win" the money for the new bedroom suite.

Mom thought it was a pipe dream, but it sounded like fun. Dad sweetened the pot by telling Janeen they could bring her sister, Carla, along for the ride. So off they went. We boys were left home with a sitter. It was one night only; that's all they could afford. So they gambled like crazy. Dad parked himself at a blackjack table; the sisters hit the slots and some cards, too. Around midnight, they weren't making much progress—breaking even or starting to lose— so they decided to turn in and go to bed. The hotel room had a queen and a couch. The sisters took the bed, which left Dad on the sofa that fit him even worse than the bed back home. He told them he'd be back in a bit and returned to the casino.

Mom and Carla were startled awake at 2 a.m., when Glenn came charging in, slightly inebriated, carrying wads of $100 bills. He turned on the lights and threw the hundreds up in the air above the bed like confetti. The ladies screamed and laughed. Mom would get her bedroom suite!

The next morning Mom got up and noticed that Dad was not on the sofa. She dressed and went downstairs to find him at the coffee shop next to the casino. His head was down; he didn't look too good. She sat down next to him. "The money?" she asked. He just shook his head. He had lost it all and was humiliated. "We are gonna get that bedroom suite, though," he said as he looked up. "We're going to charge it."

That was *not* like Dad. He had never charged anything, and Monroe had warned him to never to buy on credit. But Dad wasn't going to disappoint my mom, and he felt terrible about losing the money. So he charged the suite when he got home and bought my mom just what she had wanted. But he hated owing money.

With the bills piling up, Glenn got a second job refereeing high school basketball games after school. He had no prior experience other than his love for the game and his 6'4" frame. Glenn, nonetheless, managed to sweet-talk his way into the San Antonio referee league. It paid well, it was after hours, and it was a lot of fun.

As always, Glenn did well in his new job, and the players respected him. He was fair, but he could be tough, too—and no one messed with Glenn Patterson. Pretty soon, he was being asked to referee many of the major games in town. Glenn even considered the possibility of a career path as a referee, moving up through the college circuit and maybe even to the NBA. But it was a slow ride to get there, and the numbers didn't quite add up. He took and passed the GMAT, to open the possibility of applying to grad school. Glenn figured getting a master's degree in education would allow him to move his way up the Texas school system and one day become a principal. But his heart just wasn't in it.

The bill pile, meanwhile, kept on growing and growing.

And things took a sinister turn in terms of our feeling of personal safety. Someone shot out our porch light from across the street with a .22 while we were coming home in the dark one night. It was really creepy. They never caught who did it.

Then we were burglarized. Three times. I was too young, of course, to register any of this, but it was traumatic for Robert. Coming back to a trashed house—smashed window, drawers overturned, closets ransacked. Once, twice. And then a third time. It had become almost weirdly casual: "Oh, look, we've been robbed again ..." But Robert felt sick to his stomach. They'd taken the TV Robert had in our room—yet they forgot to grab the remote. So that's what we were left with. A remote control. It was so depressing.

Every time it happened, we had been out of town, back in Snyder for a visit with family. The San Antonio police detective had a hunch it was someone who knew we'd be away. He was right: the serial burglar turned out to be one of my mom's acting students, the troubled kid who clearly needed to create a lot of drama.

Around this time, Glenn had his second epiphany while back in Snyder for the holidays. He was having some Thanksgiving turkey with his brother-in-law, Cloyce Talbott, who'd married Glenn's older sister, Anita. Cloyce had a round face, big glasses, and a perpetual grin, even when he was mad. A real smooth talker, he could make the phone book sound interesting—not the kind of guy you'd want to sit across from at a card table. He could sell you anything. And that's just what he was trying to do, on this particular evening, to Glenn. Cloyce was a seasoned oilman already and was ready for more.

"Got a proposal for you," he grinned. "How about you and I go into business?"

"Doing what?" asked Glenn, who, in his own way, was just as wily as Cloyce.

"Drilling," Cloyce shot back.

Glenn took it in, his mind racing a million directions. Going back to the oil field was the last thing he wanted to do. But was he flattered? Absolutely. Cloyce was 10 years older and pretty impressive: he'd earned a BS in petroleum engineering from Texas Tech, and he had worked, right after graduation, for Standard Oil, where he developed enough business acumen to launch his own start-up in 1962, just four years out of school. Cloyce called his venture Snyder Well Servicing, in honor of the town he loved. He had great relationships in Snyder and decent credit with the local banks. Go down the checklist of attributes needed in a great business partner and Cloyce had 'em all. And what did Glenn have?

"We're flat broke, Cloyce," said my father.

"Don't need your money," Cloyce smiled. "Just your brains, your brawn, and your name—you see, we're calling it Patterson Drilling." Cloyce had it all figured out.

He needed an impressive front man. And Glenn had knowledge and skills that complimented those of Cloyce, who was more of a top-down management guy, whereas my father knew the oil field from the bottom up. He was a hard worker and a great leader of men.

Glenn and Cloyce looked each other in the eyes. Both these men had strong entrepreneurial spirits. Dad was ambitious, but not in a power and money kind of way; he just liked the idea of building something out of nothing.

"What'd ya say?" grinned Cloyce.

Dad protested and questioned the idea a few more times. He went back to San Antonio, but he kept thinking about Cloyce's offer. In the end, he decided men a lot dumber than the two of them were making a fortune in oil.

He called Cloyce a few days later and said, "Why the hell not?" He quit his teaching job the next day.

Chapter 5

RIVERS OF BLACK GOLD

A single oil well—Spindletop, in southeastern Texas—ushered in the modern age of petroleum. The year was 1901. Everything had been running on coal before Spindletop; steamships, locomotives, they all burned coal. Gas-powered automobiles existed at the time, but they were considered a novelty, a luxury item. Not for the masses. There just wasn't enough fuel around to power a nation of cars. Most of the limited oil exploration in the United States up to this point had been in Pennsylvania, where John D. Rockefeller's Standard Oil had a virtual monopoly, but a few maverick wildcatters were also poking around in Texas. A one-armed mechanic and self-taught geologist named Patillo Higgins was one of them. He'd been eyeing a curious hill just south of Beaumont, formed by a subterranean salt dome: an underground mound-like formation that had been pressing upward. It had Patillo wondering, What's causing all that pressure from below?

It was a hunch. There were no seismic readings you could take back in 1901, let alone the enhanced imagery we pull down these days from satellites. A hundred years ago, prospectors used pendulums, trusted what they felt in their gut, and prayed. For Patillo, it was his nose. At Spindletop, he could just smell the oil.

He wanted desperately to drill and find out, but Patillo couldn't very well do it alone, especially missing one arm. So he found a wildcatter partner in Captain Anthony F. Lucas, a retired officer from the Austrian navy who'd done a little salt mining in Louisiana and had some training in engineering. The unlikely duo shook hands—just like Glenn and Cloyce. They hired a crew and began drilling. But it was tough sledding, at first.

It took them two months to drill 800 feet. One of the issues was that they were drilling through sand, not rock, which drillers prefer; it may be harder on your bits, but it makes for a more stable well. With sand, the well would constantly cave in on itself. And these guys were facing hundreds of feet of sand. The challenge forced them, by necessity, to innovate: they invented a drilling solution we still use to this day.

Before Spindletop, drillers would pump water down the hole to flush out the cuttings produced by the drill. But desert sand and water make a slushy mess; they're not viscous enough to be efficiently extracted. The drillers needed a way to make the sand stickier so they could pull it up. So one-armed Patillo Higgins looked up at the stars one night and thought, What if we created a muddy slurry of earth and water in just the right consistency and pumped *that* down into the well? Maybe stickier mud would help to bind the sand.

It did. In fact, the idea worked miracles.

Not only did mud prove helpful in retrieving the cuttings but also it was found to stick to the sides of the hole to keep it from caving in. It allowed them to drill through the remaining sand stratum in a week and finally make progress. On January 10, 1901, the Spindletop crew hit a depth of 1,000 feet or so and paused to change out some equipment.

It began with a curious flow of mud bubbling to the surface ...

Moments later, six tons of four-inch drilling pipe shot out of the ground with tremendous force! Then nothing. A moment of eerie silence. The drillers looked at each other in confusion.

Suddenly, with the sound of 10 cannons, a geyser of mud and debris rocketed out of the hole, followed by a loud belch of natural gas and a gushing fountain of midnight black. It soared 150 feet into the air, dwarfing the derrick tower. No one had seen anything like it. The world's first gusher.

The flow did not abate. Not six hours later, not six days. It spewed out black gold like a fire hydrant on steroids for nine straight days, until they finally managed to cap that well. That single well had released close to a million barrels of oil, which was more than *all* the other wells in North America combined. (The lost oil alone would've been worth close to $50 million today.)

The sheer power of gushers like Spindletop gives you a sense of the immense subterranean pressures in these underground reserves. It's how oil was formed in the first place: the fusion by heat and pressure of organic matter, mostly from plants and algae on the ocean floor. This living matter becomes fossilized over millions of years into a dense carbon-based material—hence the term "fossil fuels."

Humans have used oil for millennia. Long before modern drilling, oil gurgled naturally to the surface through fissures in certain rock formations, and indigenous people used it as a way to waterproof their canoes.

For most of the nineteenth century, coal power was the main driver of the Industrial Revolution. Oil was used here and there for lamps and lubrication. But that all changed after Spindletop. Suddenly, petroleum replaced coal as the major fuel for new inventions like the airplane and automobile. Ships and trains that had previously run on coal power now began to switch to oil, which would soon be driving every sector of our economy. Beaumont's population skyrocketed from 10,000 to 50,000, and by 1902, there were 400 wells on that salt dome, with more than 500 Texas corporations doing business there. Many of the major oil companies were born at Spindletop, including Texaco, Gulf, Exxon, and Sun Oil.

But here's the irony. The result of the Spindletop oil glutting the market was that the price for crude dropped from $2 to 25 cents per barrel—and people lost their shirts. That's the nature of the business: wild fluctuations in price, crazy ups and downs. You gotta love roller coasters to be an oilman. It's like riding a bull.

When my father shook hands with Cloyce Talbott in 1977—75 years, give or take, after Spindletop—he'd neither ridden a bull nor stomached a roller coaster. But he was about to get on the ride of his life.

It began on an upswing. At least, it was supposed to.

Oil prices were nearing an all-time high. People were drilling anywhere and everywhere, because we were in the middle of our first "energy crisis"—a term that had just entered the American lexicon. With all eyes on Watergate, no one had been particularly focused on the Middle East when Arab forces launched a sneak attack on Israel in 1973. The normally vigilant Israelis were caught off guard; they were celebrating Yom Kippur, the holiest day in the Jewish calendar. It also happened to be during the Islamic holy month of Ramadan. Nobody was expecting Egyptian tanks to be rolling across the Sinai Peninsula while Syrian forces attacked Israel from the north.

Israeli forces mobilized fairly quickly and repelled the invaders. But when the U.S. jumped to take Israel's side, Arab states answered with another surprise: the weaponization of oil.

OPEC, the Organization of Petroleum Exporting Countries, which consists mostly of Muslim nations, announced an oil embargo against the United States, and oil prices quadrupled from $3/barrel to $12. For the first time in American history, there were long lines at the pump. We'd become complacent since World War II, when the United States once produced two-thirds of the world's petroleum. Now America was fully dependent on foreign oil, and the embargo caused pandemonium. The Arabs had us over a barrel—a barrel of oil, to be exact. Every aspect of our economy depended on readily available, relatively inexpensive gasoline, which was now being rationed at every gas station in every town across America. There just wasn't enough to go around. People had to limit time in their cars. Congress enacted a 55-mph speed limit to decrease consumption. And they passed a flurry of incentives, including tax breaks and subsidies, to stimulate domestic drilling.

Patterson Drilling, as its name squarely implied, was providing just that service. Cloyce and Glenn thought they had picked the perfect time to launch their company. But a start-up is a start-up is a start-up. It's never easy. Things had changed quite a bit since one-armed Patillo and his Austrian captain had hit the jackpot with Spindletop. The business had trifurcated into three sectors—exploration and production, drilling, and well servicing—offered by three distinct types of companies. Exploration companies, like Standard Oil, Gulf, or Texaco, were the ones with the geologists and engineers constantly on the lookout for new places to drill, using soil and seismic tests, along with other technologies. Based on their surveys, the exploration companies then negotiate leases on public and private land for mineral extraction rights. These can be costly and highly speculative, so exploration companies need a lot of cash. They also stand to make the most in success, since they get to refine and monetize all the oil they extract.

Exploration companies contract with drilling companies to actually create and drill the well and with energy service companies to keep it operational. Halliburton is the biggest and best known of these service companies. Basic Energy Services, where I am CEO, is another. This specialization in the oil business into three phases has increased efficiency and yields.

But back in the Spindletop era, those wildcatters did it all; they had to be businessmen, prospectors, amateur geologists, mechanics, engineers, and tool pushers all rolled into one or two guys. They were drilling to much shallower depths, however. Whereas Spindletop was just over 1,000 feet deep, these days we can often expect to drill 20 times that depth and even more sometimes, including horizontally.

The average well depth when my father and Cloyce hung out their shingle as Patterson Drilling was about a mile or so—a fairly manageable proposition. But there was one problem: Glenn had never done it before. Not start to finish, anyway. My father had been part of his dad's "rat hole" operation, the guys who begin the well and get the site ready for the drilling rig. He'd also done some roughnecking here and there for other drilling companies at various points of the process, but as a regular hand, not the boss. Cloyce's experience was mainly in exploration work and well servicing, which begins after the drilling is done: installing the pump jack, maintaining the flow, and eventually plugging and abandoning the well. But drilling can be the hardest part, especially when you hit a snag—which is always.

You could be half a mile down and get bogged down in a tight rock formation; your drill bit could wear out or break apart, rendering it inoperable. To replace the bit, you now have to put the drilling operation on hold and extract half a mile of piping—that means pulling out and hoisting 28, 90-foot lengths, then attaching a new bit and putting those 28 lengths of pipe back in the hole. In those days it could cost you several hours or half a day, easily. If you were to get a stuck drill pipe, you might fight it for days. Some days, the drill pipe shears, or twists off. Now you've got to go fishing for the "fish," the broken piece of pipe. Back then, you fished as long as the oil company could stomach it, or the driller, if the contract was by the foot. Drilling contracts back in the early Patterson days were mostly "footage," that is, paid by the foot, not by the day, like it is today, where the oil company assumes most of the risk of unforeseen delays. They would make around 10–15 bucks every time they drilled down another 12 inches, no matter how long it took them to do so—meaning drilling companies assumed most of the operational and financial risks.

Glenn and Cloyce faced another challenge in launching their start-up: they needed a rig. The cost of a new rig had soared to over a million bucks in 1978, which was out of the question. They'd have to find a used rig. Problem was that every decent rig was out in the field, drilling for oil. No one was selling many functional rigs in the crazy 1970s upturn. The only rigs on the market were the clunkers that no one wanted.

Cloyce found out about one such rig for sale. But it was in Bowie, almost four hours away. Glenn didn't mind the drive. (Everything in Texas is a four-hour drive.) The sun was just about setting when Cloyce and Glenn pulled up to a dusty field outside Bowie. They climbed out and looked up at the rig. It was in pieces—the whole rig would have to be assembled and refurbished. It needed a lot of work, but it was a decent rig.

"This thing's just about worthless," said Cloyce.

"Yep. Let's buy it," said Glenn.

He knew the whole thing would have to be rebuilt. But that's exactly the type of challenge he loved: making "a little something," Dad would say, "out of a whole lot of nuthin'."

Cloyce haggled the seller down to $300,000 or so, which they borrowed from a group of private investors in Snyder. Now they had to load the disassembled rig onto trucks and move it to a rented yard, where they could rebuild it. Glenn brought in his dad, Monroe, who knew a good bit about rusted iron. They also recruited some other friends and family. And the team got to work, taking apart the motors, sandblasting the derrick, priming, painting, inspecting the pipe, lubricating joints. Meanwhile, Cloyce poked around for their first drilling contract—something local, he hoped. But what he found was a job all the way back down in Victoria, near the Gulf Coast.

Finding the first job was fairly simple. Everyone was drilling—and they were drilling everywhere. Refurbishing the rig, well … that was a lot more complicated.

For one, it proved near impossible for Glenn to get the spare parts he needed. Patterson was too small a fish. There were more than 2,600 rigs in operation across North America in 1978, running 24-7 to drill the deeper holes we now needed to access our unexplored reserves. Breakdowns happened on a daily basis, and these working rigs always got priority access to the limited supply of spare parts—especially when those rigs were part of a larger fleet. A bigger fish with greater clout.

Cloyce knew the importance of scale in the oil business. But he was starting to have doubts. How was Patterson ever going to acquire a fleet when they were having trouble getting a single miserable rig to work?

It took every ounce of ingenuity my father, *his* father, and the others could collectively muster to get the damn thing operational.

They jerry-rigged stuff, welded their own parts, created work-arounds—and, finally, Rig One was up and running.

Then there was more good news: Cloyce had managed to round up their first customer, an oilman named John R. Thompson, who also happened to be one of the original Patterson investors. John R. had an oil lease that he needed drilled in Victoria, Texas, so why not hire Patterson to do it? It would be a win-win, right?

Thrilled to have their first client, Dad and his team disassembled Rig One to load it onto trucks and drive it to the drilling site about 175 miles away.

Well, something happened to Rig One as it rattled along that highway—because when they rigged it on-site, nothing worked. And I mean nothing. Whatever duct tape and bailing wire they'd used to get it running in the yard had come apart. Dad looked around in deflation and turned to the one man he could trust to turn things around: Monroe.

My father asked my grandfather a simple question: Can we fix this thing?

Monroe finished rolling a cigarette. He lit up and took a long pull.

"Way I figure is there's good news and bad news," he said, exhaling. "The bad news is nothing on this rig is working the way it's supposed to."

My father nodded. *And ...?*

"The good news is nothing else can break," said my grandfather. And he turned back to the yard. "Let's git to work."

And they went at it: more hammering, jerry-rigging, welding, lubricating. At one point the client showed up, which was very awkward, since—as a Patterson investor—he had reason to be doubly concerned. I'm sure John R. was thinking: "My God, these guys can't even drill a single well. How are they *ever* gonna build a company?"

Somehow, by hook, crook, and certainly *not* by the book, Glenn and team managed to get Rig One to start drilling. It creaked and groaned, it shook, it rattled—but soon enough, they added a length of drill pipe, then another. They were making progress!

Cloyce watched them drill for a couple of days. He nodded in satisfaction to Glenn, who was clearly relieved. Then, off he went in search of Rig Two (and a new bank loan to finance it). After Cloyce left, Rig One ran into a series of problems; it's par for the course for any rebuilt rig's first well. Burned motors with low torque, pumps requiring constant work. My father was doing his best under tough circumstances. But I have a hunch he thought more than once, What the hell have I gotten myself into?

They were losing money daily. Based on the pace they were drilling, Patterson lost more money operating the rig and paying crew than the money they received in the drilling contract. John R. Thompson left the site with mixed feelings. At least he was getting his well drilled, albeit slowly—but he was starting to think he had invested in Bad Luck Drilling, I imagine.

Cloyce was convinced the key to success lay in adding rigs and creating economies of scale that would make Patterson more competitive. For example, you could buy parts and supplies for 10 rigs cheaper on average than one.

So, with Glenn still struggling with Rig One in Victoria, Cloyce found another down in Bowie from the same source. Except this time, he said he had found a real piece of junk. Rig Two needed even more refurbishment than Rig One, and Glenn now needed to be putting out fires in two places that were six hours apart and even farther from San Antonio, which took a toll on company morale.

These men were lonely; they missed their wives and kids. Especially my dad.

Mom had stayed put in San Antonio with Robert and me. "I'm not moving back to Snyder," she had said unequivocally to Glenn when he shook hands with Cloyce Talbott at the end of 1977. We had moved to a better part of town by then, and Janeen was starting to like the idea of a simple life spent teaching school. She wasn't crazy about Glenn going back to roughnecking. It was backbreaking work, and it was dangerous. She knew she'd never see him, nor would us kids. Staying in San Antonio put her closer to Victoria, at least. Dad would be less than two hours' drive when he was at the working rig. But it was still brutal.

"We lost $800,000 in those first two years." Cloyce will tell that story to this day. He's proud of it. Not about the business disaster aspect—he's proud of the fact that they didn't throw in the towel. It would have been easy to say, Oh well, we messed up, and declare bankruptcy. But they didn't. They stuck it out. In fact, it made them stronger. Glenn and Cloyce ruled out bankruptcy during the crashes because it would have hurt too many people in Snyder, where they eventually moved most of their rigs to take advantage of the Permian Basin exposure. All of their seed money had come from local investors and local banks.

At some point, Mom decided finally to leave her teaching job in San Antonio and move us back to Snyder to be with Dad. Monroe had sat her down one day and said, "You best be moving back to be with your family." He knew that Glenn needed her support, even if he'd never admit it. Paw-Paw had gone through his own share of rough patches, and he knew the importance of sticking together in the bad times.

Glenn was thrilled to have his family back in Snyder. In response, he and Cloyce decided to move both rigs back to the Permian Basin in West Texas. They missed being local. And it proved to be the perfect move—for the family and the company. The Permian was on fire in the early '80s. Rig One and Rig Two were quickly put to work. Rig One made money, but it was a small rig. Rig Two was the more efficient driller and really turned the corner for the company back in West Texas. All of a sudden, Patterson found itself in a positive cash flow.

Once, an engineer came out to Rig Two to inspect it on behalf of the client. He wasn't impressed. My great uncle Ralph Blair, one of two or three of my dad's uncles who pushed tools, was the tool pusher at the time. The engineer told Ralph that Rig Two didn't have enough hydraulic horsepower to reach the total depth of the well.

"Hydraulic what?" said Ralph. It was obvious he didn't like the comment.

"Sonny boy," he told the button-down engineer, "you get your ass back to the office. You come back in eight days. We will be needin' to run casing at total depth by then." Eight days later the well was done, and no one challenged Ralph on what Rig Two could do anymore. Ralph taught my dad a lot about drilling wells in those first few years. Dad would later say that without him, they probably wouldn't have made it.

So two rigs became three, three became five. And Patterson became a hometown favorite, giving jobs to anyone in Snyder who needed work. Dad had hired his high school pals Donnie Newman and Robert Sterling, both of whom had served in Vietnam. They were driving all over the state at this point: eight plus hours south to their rig around Victoria, eight hours back, maybe the same night. Three hours to Midland and back, sometimes twice in the same day when a rig's in crisis. Plus they'd be working their tails off when they got on-site, with minimal breaks. They were exhausted. And the driving was killing them.

My father had a few scares where he fell asleep at the wheel— I mean literally sleeping, practically snoring. His pickup actually drove itself for a couple of white-knuckle beats before he snapped awake and thanked his lucky stars.

It was the wee hours, thank God, with no one else on the road.

One night, around midnight, Glenn found himself in South Texas, where he had procured some desperately needed spare parts for one of their Permian rigs and a pickup that was needed in the Permian as well. Glenn had flown in with Robert Sterling, who had worked his way up to Patterson vice president at this point. And Dad couldn't have been happier about it.

In the yard they called them the "Twin Towers." That was a fitting nickname as far as I was concerned. They looked like giants to me. Robert, at 6'5", had an inch on my father. But they were half that height when they'd first met! My father and Robert had both grown up in Ira, a little town right outside of Snyder. They'd played together as kids. And here they were 40 years later in a different kind of sandbox—covered in grease in an oil field halfway across Texas.

The Twin Towers certainly had their share of fun along the way. One story I'll never forget is when they were young and loose without wives in Vegas. It was the early years of Patterson, when things were looking up. I can't tell you how much my father enjoyed going to Vegas in good times or bad.

He loved the chance to invite his boyhood pal, Robert Sterling, to Vegas. They were staying in a penthouse suite at the Golden Nugget, which had given Dad VIP status at this point.

Imagine what a hoot that must have been for two scruffy boys who had grown up together in abject poverty in tiny Ira, Texas.

After a good amount of gambling and a good amount of drinking, the Twin Towers decided they were ready to turn in. So they piled into the penthouse elevator, laughing and being rather loud. Just as the doors were about to close, a giant paw came in and opened the elevator. In walked two large bodyguards in dark sunglasses, followed by a very small celebrity, also in dark shades—even though it was way past midnight.

It didn't take long for Glenn and Robert to figure out who it was: Sylvester Stallone, who stands 5'10"—so the Twin Towers towered over him. They even had a few inches on his bodyguards, who could sense that the two rednecks from Texas were fairly liquored up. There was silence during the elevator ride, which seemed to take forever. Dad was worried about what Robert might do. Since coming back from Vietnam, Robert's "give-a-shit" factor was rather low. Sure enough his fears proved correct.

"Bones!" Robert whispered in a voice that wasn't a whisper at all. (Bones was Dad's nickname from high school when his growth spurt from 5-foot-nothing to 6'4" had begun. As a freshman, he was literally "skin and bones.") Dad ignored him. He knew Robert had recognized Stallone and was about to say something stupid.

"Bones!" Robert whispered even louder—but there was zero whisper to it.

"What?" Dad whispered back—a real whisper.

"That's Rocky!" Robert whisper-shouted again. The two bodyguards were shifting a little uneasily at the two large Texans behind them discussing their boss.

"Yep," Dad whispered back. That seemed to suffice Robert for the moment and they rode in silence. But Robert kept staring at

Stallone and trying to make sense of it. About a floor or two from being at the penthouse, Robert suddenly blurted out, "He's a little bitty shit, ain't he?"

Oh damn, thought Glenn. The bodyguards turned, and Stallone turned—but he had a big grin on his face, and he started to laugh, which made the bodyguards join their boss in laughter, which made Glenn laugh, and even Robert started laughing. So the doors opened and everyone spilled out, cracking up. No one could hold it together. It said a lot about Stallone that he was able to laugh at himself like that.

He must get that a lot. These movie stars seem larger than life when they're projected up on a 30-foot screen. It's hard to fathom that Tom Cruise is only 5'7" and tough guy Sly Stallone—the guy who plays Rocky and Rambo—is not much taller. It probably provokes guys to want to try and mess with him, hence the bodyguards. That's what had worried them (and Dad) about Robert. But when everyone realized that the hammered Texans, despite their height, were harmless, it made for a big laugh.

It was a story that Glenn and Robert never forgot, and it deepened the bond between them, which brings us back to that late night in South Texas, when the Twin Towers were loading up that pickup truck with spare parts that were urgently needed back at the yard, meaning one of them had to drive that truck six hours home to Snyder.

It was way after hours, and there was no one else around. They'd flown down in a small plane that Cloyce had recently purchased; it would have been impossible to have rigs spread across Texas without one. But Glenn insisted on being the one to drive the pickup home. They were both tired. That's why Glenn instructed Robert to take the plane. But Robert knew his boss and good friend was just as trashed as he was—plus Glenn was urgently needed back at the office.

So Robert put his foot down. "I'm drivin'," he told Glenn. "You're flyin'."

Glenn caved—and regretted it for the rest of his life.

"Pull over the moment you feel tired," he had told his friend, handing him cash for a motel. Robert assured him not to worry. He dropped Glenn off at the airstrip, where the pilot was waiting. Glenn fell asleep within 10 seconds of liftoff. It took Robert a little longer.

About two hours into the drive, he pulled over to catch some sleep. There were no motels in the area, so Robert apparently slept in the car on the side of the highway in a rest area. After a few hours, he woke up—maybe roused by a semi thundering past him. Robert rubbed his eyes, took another swig of coffee, which was certainly lukewarm at that point, and then he put the pickup in gear and pulled onto the highway.

It happened in an instant. The 18-wheeler that was barreling past him just couldn't stop. The pickup was demolished, and Robert was killed instantly.

My father was devastated by the news and felt guilty that he hadn't insisted on being the guy behind the wheel. Robert had a family with small kids. Dad took care of them financially, as best he could. But it could never make up for their loss. He was haunted by Robert's untimely death for years. It shaped Dad's outlook on life somewhat.

I remember once during this time, we pulled into the Patterson yard, and there was a pickup from Ringo Drilling or one of the other Patterson competitors. I don't remember exactly which one— but the scene that unfolded I won't soon forget.

There was a tension in the yard as Dad climbed out of his truck and walked over to the competitor. The Patterson hands stopped what they were doing to watch. It was like a Western. The guy was tall like Dad, wearing jeans and boots, too, and he tipped his hat. I watched from the truck cab as my father talked to him. It didn't matter to Dad that he was a competitor. He gave him a warm handshake, asked him about his family. A few pleasantries were exchanged, then they got down to business. It looked like the guy needed a favor. Glenn listened attentively. The competitor, apparently, was having trouble procuring a spare kelly for his rig—a kelly is hexagonal piece of heavy wall pipe that transmits rotation to the drill pipe and, subsequently, the drill bit. Kellys are specially manufactured and expensive. Their kelly had failed, and drilling was stalled without a new one, so they were hemorrhaging money. Dad signaled one of the yard hands to load up a spare kelly on his competitor's trailer. They set a fair price, shook hands on it, and that was that. The Patterson crew loaded the kelly on the trailer, and off Dad's competitor went.

I couldn't believe what I'd just witnessed. When Dad walked back to the pickup, I said: "Doesn't that guy work for—" I wasn't able even to complete the sentence.

"He needed help," said Glenn, putting the Chevy in gear.

"But he's your competitor!" I blurted.

"He needed help," repeated my father. It was as simple as that.

He remembered what it felt like to be in that guy's shoes—like the time they were scrambling to get parts for Rigs One and Two and no one would help. Glenn and Cloyce were convinced that there was another way to do business, where all ships can rise. Mind you, the whole market was skyrocketing at the time. I remember wondering whether Dad would have been as generous in a crash.

A nosedive is the thing that really tests you. And one was right around the corner. That's when I'd get a chance to observe my father's true character up close.

Chapter 6

WHAT GOES UP ...

To be clear: my father was the most competitive man I have ever met.

He never let me win at basketball. Not once. He'd built our backyard hoop out of 5" drill pipe. Set it in concrete, welded a backboard onto it. That hoop could've withstood a Category 5 hurricane. I liked to shoot baskets as a break from homework on the weekends. Every now and then, Dad might be home. He'd be driving up with supplies in his truck or something. He'd see me and walk over. Watch for a moment. Then, he just couldn't help himself.

"Wanna play some one-on-one?" he'd ask. I'd jump at it.

Just so you get a complete picture, I'm a kid in shorts and sneakers. Dad, pushing 40, is wearing his standard blue jeans, ostrich boots, leather belt, and a tucked-in button-down shirt, usually plaid.

Dad didn't change for the one-on-one. He got in there right away in his boots and long pants. The shirt got untucked after a few points. Pretty soon, a button would go flying and he'd be covered in sweat. He wasn't as fast, of course, in the boots—but he had a solid foot on me. I was as determined to win as he was. And he'd let me think I had a shot at it. If we were playing to 10, Dad would let me get up to 9-5, then come back and pound me. In games of Horse or Pig, he'd let me get a few letters, then start sinking a series of impossible shots to spell the word first. That's how he was with his own son. And it's how he approached his business.

In Vegas, it was the same. He'd partner up with Cloyce regularly, sometimes a foursome with the wives. They did it often. Anita and Mom would play as hard as the men. It was fun, and it was serious, but, most of all, it had nothing to do with oil and gas drilling.

Dad liked the thrill of winning, and he loved the competitiveness. He liked being treated like a big shot—because he'd never experienced that in his life. He liked the golf, the shows, the food; he liked it all. But as he became more successful, the thing he appreciated the most of all, I think, was the distraction. No phones were ringing for him at the Golden Nugget. He'd sit and play blackjack for hours and hours. He loved the total mindlessness of Vegas, where he could have fun and not be bothered. I understand because I've experienced this same feeling—the need to get your mind off of the utter hell of running a struggling business and just play cards. It is truly a getaway. Win or lose.

Don't get me wrong; Dad wanted to win, and he hated to lose. I'm the same way. But what was remarkable about Dad is that he usually gave away almost as much as he was winning. He was always a very generous man. He loaned money to all kinds of people and never expected it back. To expect it back was not a true loan, in his mind. Nowhere did this generosity manifest itself more so than in Vegas.

One night, late for dinner reservations, Glenn decided impulsively to play the quarter slots on their way out, and, wouldn't you know it—he scored a jackpot! A casino employee handed him a bucket, which quickly filled up with an avalanche of change. Glenn knew that if he went to have the coins counted and exchanged for bills, they'd miss their dinner reservations, which would disappoint Anita and Janeen, who were waiting for him with Cloyce.

Anita said, "We are going to be late if you cash that bucket in!"

Dad said, "No problem."

So Glenn carried the bucket of quarters to the car instead, handing out fistfuls of quarters to everyone he passed. Pitching them in fountains and stacking them on statues. In the limo they had rented to drive them to dinner, Dad started tossing the coins to people in the streets. A few yelled back, "Thanks!" Dad yelled back, "See you same time tomorrow!" By the time they got to the restaurant, the bucket was empty and everyone was laughing and enjoying the evening.

But it wasn't only after winning a jackpot that Dad acted generously in Las Vegas. Whether Dad was winning or losing, he'd come slide money under your hand, and if he won, he'd just pull his original bet back and give you the winnings. If he lost, he'd do it again until he won. And you'd get to keep the winnings. He'd call it a "starter kit." Something to get you going.

Dad loved Vegas. He loved the distraction.

* * *

By the early 1980s, Patterson had five working rigs.

"On our way to a bona fide fleet," brimmed Cloyce in obvious satisfaction. His next idea: offer stock in Patterson to raise sufficient cash so they could expand even more. Glenn thought it was a good plan, and they started offering shares in Patterson at five bucks a pop. It was not too difficult to get their friends to commit to the first 20,000 shares, along with a number of other local investors, for a total raise of $1 million. There seemed to be no shortage of people willing to bet on Patterson. Cloyce and Glenn had respect within the community; drilling was booming. A seed investment in Patterson seemed rock-solid. There was only one problem. From a legal standpoint, it was not the proper way to raise funds. (You're not allowed to sell significant numbers of shares of a company that hasn't been registered with the SEC.)

Both Cloyce and Glenn were clueless about that particular securities regulation at the time, so they had to file a lot of retroactive paperwork at their eventual IPO in 1993. But in the early days, "paperwork" was a four-letter word at Patterson. You did business with a handshake or, sometimes, a note scrawled on a napkin. My father was allergic to computers. He was even averse to flip phones, let alone smartphones. I remember when he finally gave up his hard-mounted truck phone for a "bag" phone. He called it the "nag" phone. Then he had to give that up for the flip phone. He was always the last guy to upgrade. He preferred making contact by looking you in the eye. That's the way Glenn did his business. And so did Cloyce.

So they never bothered to register with the SEC. It never even occurred to them. (Those seed investors eventually cleaned up BTW, earning 15–30 times their original investment if they stayed with it.) And, in 1984, Cloyce and Glenn decided to change the name of their company from Patterson Drilling to Patterson Energy, with plans to expand into exploration, along with drilling. Cloyce had been investing in oil leases for years as a side business. And he invited my father into a couple of deals after they formed Patterson Petroleum. Now, with opportunities abounding, they were hoping to steer the company into the exploration sector, too.

But the price of oil had started to level off, even slide a few points, just like in the aftermath of Spindletop. The flurry in domestic drilling in the late 1970s eventually caused a glut in supply, which depressed global oil prices. And there was a double whammy this time: sharply elevated prices from the embargo had had a dampening effect on demand, too. People worldwide had changed their behavior patterns around gasoline consumption—governments, too.

The cost for a barrel of crude, which peaked at an all-time high of $38 in 1980, fell steadily for the next several years. By 1985, oil had fallen to $26, which was still an order of magnitude greater than where prices had been before OPEC announced its embargo in 1973. The Arab member nations had netted trillions of dollars during that time period, and they wanted the party to go on forever, especially Saudi Arabia, which had been the world's largest producer of petroleum. (The Russians, in response to the OPEC embargo, steadily increased their oil production, and now they ranked number one in total output.)

OPEC countries still controlled one-third of the world's supply, which was more than enough to move the market when they worked in tandem. The Saudis had been urging fellow OPEC members to limit their output in order to keep prices high. But no one paid them heed. With prices still 10 times greater than where they'd been a decade earlier, countries like Iraq and Kuwait were determined to sell as much oil as they could.

By 1986, Saudi Arabia was fed up. It decided suddenly to maximize its market share by flooding the market with its reserves. The price for crude dropped to $10 per barrel, and companies stopped drilling. Patterson, now at 13 rigs, had all 13 running January 1, 1986. Ninety days later, they had none running. Not exactly the best news for a still-growing start-up.

So what did Glenn and Cloyce do? They scaled the company, laid folks off, cut wages (especially their own), and hunkered down for a crash. They also played a lot of cards. More gin rummy, to be exact. It's what they always did at the end of a workday, like a sacred ritual, rain or shine. On good days or bad days, the way to unwind was always the same: a game of gin. Or 10. Or 20. For money, in a ledger. And there was one rule: no work talk. Cause that wouldn't be "unwinding"—it'd still be work.

Cards were shuffled; business stopped. It didn't mean they stopped thinking about it; it just meant they stopped talking about it. They saved that for later. Out in the yard, walking toward the vehicle, that's when one of them would stop and turn to the other with a sudden thought.

"How about we go visit some auctions?" offered my father one evening in the late 1980s. With oil prices nearing historic lows and the crash in full swing, Glenn's idea was to double down (like he did every time he lost at cards). Cloyce loved it. They both knew that the market had to turn at some point. And, with everyone running for the exits, there were some real bargains to be had in spare parts for drilling rigs. So, with whatever money they could cobble together or borrow, Cloyce and Glenn went on a buying spree. They bought for Patterson, and they bought miscellaneous stuff together personally. They bought and sold and bought and sold.

A clutch that normally cost $5,000 was now available for $50; drill pipe was being auctioned for 10 cents on the dollar. Patterson snapped it up by the truckload. They even bought the trucks—at 5 cents on the dollar. One collapsing company offered them $5,000 worth of equipment for $5, meaning one-tenth of 1%. When Skytop Brewster, a high-end manufacturer of oil rigs, went bankrupt, Cloyce snapped up 35 trailer-truck loads of equipment worth millions new for 10 cents on the dollar—basically for the salvage cost of the metal by the pound. Rotary tables for rigs that were new and normally cost $45,000 were bought for $4,000. They stockpiled an entire warehouse of spare parts, more than enough to service all their rigs and a bunch more. They even snapped up a few extra rigs.

This auction scene of buying and selling equipment was repeated throughout Texas. Sometimes it was Cloyce, sometimes Glenn, sometimes both. They figured when the business turned around (and it always did ... at least it had before, right?), they'd be ready and nimble, while others would be covered in rust. They made money any way they could. They sold interest in some oil wells—anything to survive.

One day, Cloyce got a front-row, splash-zone view of the volcanic Glenn Patterson temper that he'd heard so much about from his wife (Glenn's sister), my aunt Anita—who'd known Dad his entire life, of course. Once you saw that foaming mouth, you'd better stand 40 feet clear. Cloyce didn't believe it.

You're exaggerating, he told Anita. Wait and see for yourself, she warned.

So Cloyce and Glenn were going down to Midland to make a collection call on a deadbeat customer who'd been avoiding them for months. There's nothing that Dad hated more than a liar and a cheat. He had no problem dealing with clients going through difficult times; as long as they were honest about it, he'd work with them. So would Cloyce. What Dad could not stand was someone who kept promising to pay an outstanding bill by a certain day but would never come through. It meant more phone calls, more promises, more bullshit: "I'm good for it," the guy would say. "You got my word, Glenn."

His word? Glenn laughed. His word was worthless. This guy was so crooked that if he swallowed a nail, he'd spit up a corkscrew. No more damn phone calls. Time for a house call. Aunt Anita got worried about what might happen to the guy in Midland if Glenn were to go alone, so she told Cloyce he had to go with him—and be careful!

Cloyce rolled his eyes. He had *never*—not once—seen Glenn out of control. It could not possibly be that bad. What was everyone so freaked out about?

So Glenn and Cloyce drove together to Midland. The trip was actually full of other business, but they might pay the guy a visit if time allowed. It did. So they showed up at the deadbeat's workplace. But it was shuttered—everyone was gone.

"He's gone bankrupt," said Cloyce.

"Doesn't mean he's gone broke," answered Glenn, who went around chatting up some of the neighbors in the building, who themselves were cagey and suspicious. Finally, someone was willing to talk: "I'm not supposed to tell you guys this, but they moved over to this other place."

The new place turned out to be an old renovated gas station: a bunch of people at desks, working the phones—meaning *not* bankrupt. Glenn strode inside and asked for the guy by name; let's call him Bob.

"Is Bob around?" he asked.

A few furtive glances. "Bob doesn't work here," someone said.

But Dad recognized a young lady: "Shirley, right? Bob's secretary, right?" I'm not sure her name was Shirley, but Dad knew her name.

It was uncanny. He had met this woman exactly once in his life, probably five years earlier, and he still remembered her name. Dad had a crazy memory for detail when it came to people's lives. And he tried to engage on that level with everyone he met. In this case, it clearly paid off—because "Shirley" had nowhere to hide. She admitted she was Bob's assistant but Bob was out of town. Glenn nodded politely and sat his lanky frame on a chair in the waiting room. Cloyce followed suit. "We'll wait."

People were starting to get edgy. Shirley insisted that Bob was "really gone," like *overnight* gone. Glenn was not budging. Sooner or later that son of a bitch was gonna show up, Dad thought. And he intended to be right here when that happened, he told the increasingly nervous Shirley. There were a few whispered exchanges, conversations behind closed doors. Then another man surfaced and said he was Bob's brother, and he asked Glenn to calm down and invited him to wait outside. He had a secret to discuss with him.

Once outdoors, Bob's brother began a sob story about how Bob dragged the whole family into his drilling schemes and they'd all lost money. He understood how Glenn felt and said they were all in this together.

Together? Glenn had to laugh. "All I want is the money he owes Patterson, then you'll never see me in this shit hole again. You— you're tied to that SOB for life."

That's when Bob drove by in a new Lincoln Continental and circled to the rear of the building. Dad yelled in delight: "Well, there's the piece of shit right there!"

Glenn took off on foot toward the rear of the building, while Cloyce and the brother ran inside and then out the back door— where Glenn had yanked Bob out of the Lincoln and pinned him by his neck to the side of the car, screaming in full froth about the money owed to Patterson. The brother tried to intervene, and Glenn ended up pinning both of them by the neck against the car. Foam had formed in the corners of his mouth; Cloyce was seeing the Patterson eruption in all its glory. There was no talking to him. But Cloyce tried anyway, playing good cop, trying to calm his partner down. Glenn finally backed off. He'd probably left bruises, but the message was delivered. He vowed to be back if the account was not settled. I believe the gentleman found some spare money to pay Patterson. He may not have paid it all, but he paid enough that he never received another white foam spit session.

Later when Dad's brother, Alton, heard the story from Cloyce, Alton asked him whether he stayed around to see any of that foam hit the ground. Cloyce said, "Well, I guess I did because I never left." Alton said, laughing loudly, "Then, Cloyce, you stayed too long. You're lucky he didn't grab you too!"

Alton had seen that foam fly a few times and knew that anyone within choking distance might get swallowed up by that rage, too. I could testify to that fact, myself.

There was another incident involving collection—this time, just Glenn, no Cloyce to buffer him. Glenn happened to be driving through Big Spring when he passed an oil lease owned by another deadbeat customer. It should have been shut down, but he noticed there was a rig up and running. It was a well-servicing rig, meaning the rig that comes in to service the well once it's been drilled. Patterson had drilled that well and never been paid for it. Dad happened to know the owner of the service rig; it was a cousin of his named Van Gastin, so he drove onto the property and told Van he should pull the rig down and leave immediately because the guy didn't pay his bills. The customer showed up and protested. He asked Glenn to leave, threatened to call the police.

Dad didn't take that too well. He decided to haul the guy into his truck and drive him 45 miles to Snyder to have him sign a note to pay Patterson back for all he owed. The guy went along and signed the note. He didn't have much choice. God only knows what they talked about during that car ride.

The next day Patterson received a letter from the guy's lawyer saying the note was no good because Dad had kidnapped the guy and forced him to sign. Furthermore, Dad was to leave the guy

alone or face court action. Dad laughed it off and said, "Oh well.
It sure was fun to see that crook squirm a little!" They never did
get paid.

* * *

By the late 1980s, Patterson pared staff down to essential personnel,
with everyone wearing multiple hats. Everyone agreed to pay cuts.
They had no choice. It was that or no job at all. Cloyce stopped
drawing a salary altogether at one point, which was really tough on
him. Dad cut his own pay to the bare minimum. This was the period
when Dad started waking us up before dawn on Saturdays to drive
to abandoned oil fields, where we'd cut pipe for resale as scrap metal
to make payments on our bank loans. The local banks, rewarding
Cloyce and Glenn for their loyalty to Snyder, were allowing them
to pay interest only, substantially reducing their monthly payments.
Dad hated being in debt and always tried to keep Robert and me
from incurring any. "Rack up too much debt and you'll be scratchin'
a broke ass," he used to say.

He had gotten the idea to cut and resell pipe by thinking about
what his dad might have done under the circumstances. Monroe,
who'd died in 1980 of lung cancer after a lifetime of smoking, had
been nicknamed "Scrap Iron" Patterson, for his penchant to collect
and recycle metal. Dad missed his father, I'm sure, during these difficult times. He thought often about the life lessons and work ethic
he'd inherited. If another Depression were to hit, we'd be fine—
Monroe would tell my dad—because we'd outhustle the next guy.
That was the Patterson legacy passed down from Monroe to Glenn
and from Glenn to Robert and me. There was *always* a way to get
by. You just needed to think of it. (Like Dad, I missed having my
father to talk to during the oil crash of 2015 and 2016.)

It was during a card game, apparently, with Donnie, not Cloyce, that Glenn put down his cards suddenly and looked off into space. "I got it!" he said.

He rose from the table with a clear vision and a plan.

"Where the heck are you goin'?" asked Donnie. "To the Polar field," smiled Glenn.

Donnie laughed. No one's drilling there anymore, he said. Exactly, said Glenn.

They were practically giving away spare parts at auction—that is, items they actually bothered to haul from the field. What about the things they left behind? Like the flow lines? There were literally tons and tons of scrap metal on any given oil field. Dad knew he could buy that Polar field stuff at damn near free—for pennies, literally. It was certainly worthless, sitting in a field, 20 miles from the nearest town. But what if you cut that pipe into manageable lengths and moved it to the yard? It suddenly has value—to build fencing in a cost-effective way, at a time when people everywhere were looking for ways to save money.

It was actually a pretty good idea, though it seemed totally whacko at the time to my 12-year-old mind. We ended up going to that field and cutting pipe more than two dozen times, making close to $100,000 all told. That and a few other schemes saved Dad's tail. And mine too, I guess.

Bottom line: even though it was one of the worst downturns in the history of oil exploration—a time when oil companies, left and right, were shuttering and laying off everyone—Patterson Energy would manage to survive.

Chapter 7

DON'T KICK
A MAN WHEN
HE'S DOWN

The brawl at the Snyder Country Club became the overnight talk of the town. I didn't witness it myself. But I sure heard about it—for years. From multiple sources, some factual, some mythologized. I wish I had seen it with my own eyes. That's the fantasy of a lot of 14-year-old boys, I bet—to see how their daddy would fare in a real, epic fistfight.

I had heard stories from Donnie, my uncle Alton, and my aunts about Dad's reputation in high school and in his early 20s—never afraid to raise his fists and pretty much undefeated. But that was a long time ago. Dad hadn't been in a fight for decades.

By 1988, tensions were running deep in towns all across the Permian Basin. Everyone was on edge, out of work. The crash was dragging on and on. People had gone bankrupt, left and right, losing their homes. It was a powder keg. There was some light at the end of the tunnel, but times were still very tough. That's when it happened.

You do not want to be on the receiving end of a whipping by Glenn Patterson—that I can tell you firsthand. Dad disciplined us with a custom-made paddle he'd been given by a fellow teacher in San Antonio. It was a Louisville Slugger that had been shaved on two sides, ripped through a table saw so that it was flat. It made the perfect paddle. The handle was still round, however, and apparently very easy for Dad to get a firm grip on. Glenn could light your ass up with that thing. And it worked. Man, that thing got your attention. He used it sparingly—to the point that you'd almost forget what it felt like and get complacent. Then—*Whammo!* You'd remember in a hurry.

Apparently, we didn't have it as bad as my father and Alton had it with their dad, Monroe, who doled out spankings all the time. He usually grabbed anything he could lay his hands on: a switch from a tree, a wooden spatula, his belt, which he'd fold in half for additional heft. The belt was the most common, apparently.

My father told us about one whipping he and Alton got (and clearly deserved) after riding their bicycles across a busy highway when they were told to get off their bikes and walk them across after looking both ways. Monroe had been working daylights on a drilling rig after the family had moved back to the Snyder area, and he knew Glenn and Alton would be crossing the highway on their bikes while he was gone to work. So he left specific instructions on how to do it safely.

"Don't you go ridin' them bikes across that road, ya hear?" was Monroe's explicit warning. "You better get off and look both ways and then walk them across!"

But Dad and Alton did what all kids do: they got in a hurry and did whatever came naturally. The highway was quiet, and their parents were at work.

Off they went. Roaring onto the asphalt, wind in their hair. They could always get their bicycles going faster on the blacktop. A feeling of total freedom and power. It lasted 30 seconds or so before they saw Monroe. He had come home early, and Glenn and Alton had pulled out right in front of him on the highway.

Oh shit, thought Glenn. We're toast.

Monroe had grabbed a willow limb of a nearby tree and was waiting for them. Alton said he and Dad peddled their bikes as slowly as they could, but they eventually arrived at home. The beating was severe. After that, neither of them wanted to ride their bikes at all for a while.

I must confess that I, too, have known a few episodes of that ilk. The first one I can remember was after I had punched a bunch of random holes in our cinder block fence, as a safe place to bury my "treasure" (a nine-year-old fantasy; not sure what I was thinking, exactly). I got a claw hammer and chiseled out a series of holes in the hollow blocks. My father was furious when he saw the willful destruction of property. That called for the paddle. Guaranteed.

Another time was when I called my mother an asshole. Not to her face, of course; I would never have done that. It was in the privacy of my own bathroom, after a terrible fight we had had over clothes she wanted me to wear. Our house, at the time, was connected by a series of air ducts. My mother heard me say "asshole" through the vent! She charged in with the paddle (Dad was away) and laid into me.

But Robert and I were accustomed to Dad's two-handed home run swings with that paddle. Mom didn't have the strength to smack us that hard. I giggled, I think. And that spelled my doom. When Glenn came home, he made damn sure I would never disrespect my mother again. You better believe I did not giggle.

But the worst incident may have been the time that my brother and I decided to make fun of the paddle itself, by adorning it with Patterson Drilling hard hat stickers and writing "Patterson Beater" on it with magic markers—neither of which could be easily removed by an infuriated Glenn, who put the newly christened Patterson Beater to immediate use.

During the tension surrounding the crash of the late 1980s, you'd think the paddle situation would have gotten worse for us. But I don't remember a lot of spankings in that era. I was on my best behavior, I guess—sensing my father was under a ton of pressure. This was the period when Dad started waking us up at 6 a.m. on a Saturday to drive out to abandoned oil fields, where we'd cut pipe all day to resell at 50 cents a foot. That day we accidentally started a five-acre brush fire, I thought for sure I was going to be getting the paddle. I felt it had been on me. It was my job to contain the sparks from the acetylene torch. But nothing happened that night. No paddle.

My dad knew I'd been hustling as fast as my little legs would carry me, stomping out flare-ups, covering them with sand. The wind was simply too strong that day. It could have happened to anybody—which brings us back to the Snyder Country Club, on a spring day in 1988. The day that Glenn Patterson had enough.

I need to set the stage. Snyder Country Club was comfortable— nothing fancy. Nine run-of-the-mill golf holes but most folks stayed inside, especially during the toasty summer months. There was a nice bar or parlor with a few tables where everyone congregated to play cards. The real thing that drew people to the country club in the evenings—let's be honest about it—was the booze. You see, Snyder—all of Scurry County, for that matter—was dry. No alcohol anywhere. The country club, being a private establishment, was one of the only places that could legally serve it. So people started gathering at happy hour and often stayed into the night, which was a harmless way to unwind during stressful times. No matter how bad it was, there's nothing you couldn't put aside with a few rounds of gin rummy and a Crown and Diet Coke or two. That's how my father felt.

Some guys skipped the cards and concentrated on the booze. Once emboldened, they'd lay in with the trash talk. Even Dad, being 6'4" and tough as hell, caught his share of it. Teasing and trash talk are fine, and Dad could dish it and take it with the best of them. But you had better not touch anybody. There had been another incident, in fact, before the legendary brawl of 1988 (which landed one guy in the hospital). A different individual had riled Glenn a few months prior. On this occasion, a guy came up behind Glenn and pulled the hair at the back of his neck. It was physical contact—the line had been crossed.

Quick as a whip, Glenn spun around and grabbed the guy, slinging him over his shoulder onto the card table! Drinks went flying, cards, ice cubes. But that was it. Glenn got up, and it ended right there, with nothing but a bruised ego.

Fast-forward six months later to spring of 1988. What started out as a pretty usual evening at the country club ended up with one particular guy and Dad exchanging some less than friendly comments. As it started up, Dad happened to be there with his buddy from high school, Donnie Newman. They were playing cards when the trash talk escalated. We'll call this other guy Rick, a 250-pound linebacker type who was as big as Dad and clearly spent some of his free time at the gym. He was accompanied by an equally beefy sidekick; let's call him Cliff.

All the men had had a few rounds of cocktails at this point, and the trash talk worsened. There was some historical discontent between Rick and Dad. I don't know all the details, but they clearly didn't care for each other. Just never clicked when they happened to be in the same circles.

More words were exchanged between Rick and Dad; things started to get ugly. Donnie and Glenn stuck to their cards, trying not to engage. But Dad decided he'd heard enough and got up from the table suddenly to head for his truck. Rick wanted to prove a point, which meant they wouldn't be backing down any time soon. It was up to Glenn to retreat, which was exactly what he did. That had its own consequences, of course—more jeers, more taunting of the "chickenshit" variety. Dad bit his lip, walked out. Rick followed Glenn out into the parking lot and gave him a shove from behind. That's when it got messy.

I'll pick up the story from my 14-year-old point of view, which began the morning after at 6 a.m., when Dad came into my room with a somber expression. It was Saturday. I was expecting we were about to go to work. But as Dad approached the bed, I saw something was wrong. His face was bruised—a laceration on his forehead, held together by a Steri-Strip.

"You're gonna hear a lot of talkin' 'bout this," said Dad. His voice was calm. "I want you to hear it from me first."

So he told me the whole story of exchanging words with Rick and things getting heated between them, how he realized pretty quickly that the only way to avoid a fight was to get the hell out of there—so he beelined for his truck, but Rick followed him out into the parking lot.

Rick shoved Dad in the back before he could get into his truck. Donnie and Rick's guest, Cliff, had come outside, too, at this point. The adrenaline was redlining.

After the shove, Dad asked him, "Are you done?" Then Rick took a swing at Dad, and all hell broke loose. Fists went flying, knees, elbows, anything. Cliff, apparently, was not there to pile on but to break things up. When he tried to intervene, however, Donnie mistook this for his jumping into the fight, and Donnie went after Cliff. Cliff, who had 50 pounds on Donnie, soon went down. Donnie cracked some ribs, and Cliff cowered away. In a subsequent telling of the story, I heard he crawled for safety under a parked Cadillac. So much for trying to break up a fight.

A few people were out in the parking lot by then to watch the show. Some had carried their drinks outside with them. It didn't get much better than that in terms of live entertainment in Snyder. This was a town where getting a new traffic light made the paper.

Rick and Glenn were fairly evenly matched. But Dad fought smart. He waited for just the right moment to land a combination that left Rick in the mud. Then Glenn returned to his truck to get out of there. But Rick didn't think they were done just yet, so he lurched into his car to give chase.

"I hurt him a little at the club; I just wanted to let him know I could," my dad explained gravely. "But I didn't finish him off."

My eyes were as wide as saucers. "When that stupid SOB went and followed me down the road, well … that's when I really whipped him. I whipped him pretty bad."

I can just imagine the scene: Dad pulling away in his truck, seeing the guy zooming up in his rearview mirror, and thinking, What the hell? The bead of white spit had no doubt formed in the corner of Glenn's mouth by then. So he slammed on the brakes and pulled over. Okay, asshole—you got yourself an ass whoopin'!

He was hopping mad, but he kept it contained, letting Rick throw the first couple of wild punches, waiting for a good opening and—BAM! Out came the fury of Glenn Patterson in full tilt. This time he didn't stop when Rick went down; Glenn kept pounding away until Rick was seeing stars and about to pass out, ready for the emergency room.

Glenn backed off finally. His knuckles hurt. He stared at Rick, flat on his back and not likely to move any time soon. Broken nose?

Busted lips? Who knows. Glenn sighed and climbed into his truck. And everybody in Snyder was soon talking about it. Once Dad calmed down, he was ashamed. He did not like that kind of attention—any attention. He had embarrassed his family, he thought. A grown damn man involved in a stupid fistfight. He was mad as hell at the whole damn episode.

He was also worried about Rick. One of my dad's closest friends named Dalton Walton heard about it early that same night; he was friends with both Rick and my dad. Dad had someone call Dalton to ask him to come over to the Patterson Drilling office, where Dad was trying to calm down. Dalton showed up at the office, where Glenn was nursing a glass of Crown and eyeing a pistol on the table—which he'd have used without hesitation had Rick come around for round 3.

After briefly cussing and discussing the fight, Dad asked Dalton a favor.

"Will you go check on Rick?" Dad said.

"Of course." Dalton had planned on going there next, anyway.

So Dalton headed over to make sure Rick was okay. He showed up at Rick's place and almost got shot. Rick was sitting there with a shotgun, waiting for Glenn while nursing some wounds, trying to ease the swelling.

"Yer lucky your name ain't Glenn Patterson," growled Rick. "I'da killed you."

Neither Rick nor Dad was taking any chances.

It's a testament to Dalton Walton that he managed to diffuse the situation between Rick and Glenn. They actually became friendly over time and buried the past. And, to my knowledge, my father never fought again. Dad, for his part, was deeply embarrassed by the fight. I can remember him making a point to speak nice of

Rick over the years to others. He respected him. Dalton once told me that Rick was very upset when he learned that Dad was ill with Alzheimer's. I guess that says a lot about both men in the end.

Left: Monroe with Glenn and Alton at dairy in Anton, Texas.

Below: Eudell, Monroe, Charlene, Anita, and Glenn in Anton, Texas.

Right: Glenn teaching Robert to shave, late 1970s.

Left: Glenn, Janeen, Robert, and Roe in San Antonio, Texas.

Below: Monroe, late 1970s.

Left: Glenn building an early Patterson drilling rig, late 1970s

Right: Rig 1.

Below: Rig 7.

Top: Janeen, Glenn, Shirley and Donnie Newman, and Lynn McLarty, Las Vegas, early 1980s.

Above: Robert Sterling, M.L. Duke (early partner in Melco), Glenn, Rusty Melton (Glenn's friend and owner of Melco), early 1980s.

Right: Rare trip to the beach for Glenn. Glenn with Troy (nephew) and Janette Allen (niece), 1980s.

Above: Glenn playing
Gin with Cloyce
while James Brown
(first CFO) looks on.

Right: 1993 Road Show,
New York City.

Left: End of the
1993 Road Show.

Right: Glenn,
James Brown,
Cloyce, and
David Lucky
(investment
banker), posing
on Wall Street
with the
Charging Bull,
1993 Road Show,
New York City.

Left: Glenn, Anita, Cloyce, and Roe in Las Vegas after Anita hit a jackpot that saved us all that trip.

Below: Alton, Charlene, Anita, and Glenn, early 2000s.

Glenn and Janeen (center), with Roe and Tonya (left), Robert and Angie (right), and their five grandchildren.

Above: Janeen and Glenn before Alzheimer's onset, early 2000s.

Right: Glenn just after Alzheimer's diagnosis, 2006.

Chapter 8

"CONSTRUCTIVE TOTAL LOSS"

Probably the dumbest decision they ever made—certainly the craziest—could have easily forced Patterson into bankruptcy. But, as things turned out, it ended up saving their asses.

The story began in the late 1980s, when Cloyce took a call from a man named Bob Barbanell, a lead banker at the Bank of New York, which was about as prestigious as it got. The bank had been founded in 1773 by the face on the $10 bill—Alexander Hamilton—which is why they get to have "The buck *started* here" as their slogan. It's one of the two oldest banks in America (the other being Bank of America itself).

New York is a long way from Texas. But there wasn't a bank anywhere that had avoided being hit by the oil crash. Several major financial institutions had been forced to declare bankruptcy, including Continental Illinois out of Chicago, once the seventh-largest bank in America. Seafirst Bank from Seattle and a cluster of Texas banks had also failed, including First Republic of Dallas, First City National, Gibraltar Savings out of Houston, and even the First National Bank of Midland. When the price of oil tanked, they all went belly up. Too many bad loans, too many foreclosures.

Bob Barbanell was feeling it, 1,500 miles away on Wall Street at the Bank of New York, which was recently forced to seize several rigs in foreclosure. He wanted those rigs off his books as quickly as possible, and that's why he called Cloyce Talbott.

"Word on the street is that Patterson is buying up rigs," opened Barbanell.

"Where'd y'all hear a crazy thing like that?" responded Cloyce in his Texas drawl. "Who's got dry powder these days to buy anything?" It was true. Partially. (He was also playing a little poker to lower expectations, in case Barbanell had something irresistible to offer.) But when the New York banker told him the rigs were on the Texas-Louisiana border—stacked out in the Sabine River just before the Gulf, to be exact (they were offshore oil platforms)—Cloyce put on the brakes.

"We're land drillers," said Cloyce.

"Not what I'm being told," insisted Barbanell.

Barbanell knew that Patterson had recently made a deal with another bank for some shallow-water barge rigs they'd foreclosed on and were eager to unload. (Shallow-water barges are used for offshore wells that are fairly close to the shoreline. They're essentially floating platforms that can be anchored and tethered for drilling in water depths of less than 50 feet or so.) But drilling in water, whether shallow or deep, is an entirely different animal from land drilling; it requires an entirely different skill set, bigger crews, and 24-hour operations, and it entails much more danger and 10 times the insurance. The rigs—engineered to house and feed a small army of people while also surviving weather extremes like tropical storms and hurricanes—are more elaborate and complex.

They cost barrels of money to operate and boatloads of money to buy.

The bank in the barge rig case was stuck holding a note worth $27 million for these barges, at a time when no one was buying rigs—except crazy contrarians like Cloyce and my dad. But there was a limit to their risk tolerance. The word "offshore" made them skittish. So they decided to counter with $800,000, an offer that basically said "not interested."

Far from hanging up on them, the bank accepted. And, just like that, Cloyce and Glenn were in the shallow offshore drilling business. On the advice of lawyers, they formed a subsidiary separate company with new investors, Patterson Gulf Coast, so it wouldn't bring down the whole company in case the offshore play was a total bust, which seemed like a real possibility.

Fast-forward six months later to Bob Barbanell on speakerphone from the Bank of New York, now offering a pair of offshore jack-up platforms rated for medium water depths around 1,500 feet or so: Big Foot One and Big Foot Two. These were so-called jack-up barge rigs that got towed to the drilling location by tug boats, then *jacked up* to stand up on the massive pylons that go down to the ocean floor—more expensive, more dangerous, more everything.

Glenn's gut said no way; ditto for Cloyce.

"Just take a look at them," pleaded Barbanell. "That's all I'm asking." He even offered to fly them out on the bank's dime. Glenn and Cloyce figured: What've we got to lose? So they flew to Beaumont and then took a boat out to the rigs stacked out in the Sabine River Pass on the Texas-Louisiana border. Glenn took a deep breath as he stepped out onto the impressive platform and took it all in: three gigantic legs supporting a triangular deck about 200 feet across, a towering derrick, powerful pumps, weatherproof machine room, repair shop, support infrastructure, dorms, mess hall. Wow. Glenn could certainly see how it had cost $25 million to build. And now it was in mothballs for the most part, with only a skeleton crew to keep things from completely rusting to pieces.

Even stacked rigs need to be insured for liability, however, especially when they're sitting on the Gulf Coast. Between insurance and maintenance, the Bank of New York was losing $60,000 a month hanging onto them. That's why Barbanell was so motivated to sell—at any price.

Glenn looked around: the thing was practically brand new, hardly used at all. Just how crazy was he feeling? He took a look at Cloyce, who was asking himself the same question.

The path to a solution was obvious to both of them: gin rummy.

Back home, Cloyce and Glenn observed the "No Business at the Card Table" rule, even though both of them knew they'd be getting a call from Bob Barbanell any minute now. Should they just pass this time? At a time when no one was drilling, they'd be crazy to expand Patterson Gulf Coast. Right? The last time they came back with a crazy lowball counteroffer, not even 4% of the sticker price, the damn bank accepted and they became the reluctant owners of $27 million worth of barge rigs.

Around the fifth hand of cards, they received the call from Bob, who got right to the point: "Make me an offer."

Cloyce said, "I don't want to. It'll be embarrassing for me AND for you!"

"Just make the offer," insisted the New York banker. Cloyce covered the phone while he and Dad decided on a number for just one of the platforms. No way they were doing two.

"Two hundred twenty-five thousand," said Cloyce. Less than 1% of what Big Foot was worth.

"Give me five minutes," said Barbanell. Click.

The phone rang in three: "Deal."

So Patterson Gulf Coast had a brand-new offshore jack-up. And not a damn clue what to do next. They were compelled by federal and state authorities to carry a minimum of $2 million in insurance—much more than they wanted or could afford—so they had to put the rig to work, adding 30 workers to the payroll, at a time when everyone else was laying them off.

In its first 150 days of drilling, Big Foot One lost $5,000 per day. It was a disaster.

Cloyce and Glenn were back in Snyder eating lunch at the country club one day, wondering what the hell they had gotten themselves into. Would Patterson be forced to shut its doors like so many of its competitors? Not only was the land-drilling business bad but also now they had an offshore mess on their hands. It'd be an awful outcome, one that my father was dreading, not just for himself and Cloyce but also for their original investors, who had stood by them all this time. But they'd painted themselves into a corner. They owned the damn thing. They couldn't sell it. And Big Foot was hemorrhaging their bank account. It was unsustainable. But neither Cloyce nor Glenn had any idea how to get out of this one.

As they returned to the office from lunch, they were met at the door by some agitated staff who shouted, "Big Foot is sinking!"

They hopped on their small plane to Louisiana right then and had the pilot circle the rig when they arrived. Big Foot was working in the Mississippi Delta at the time. It had keeled over at a 35° angle. One of its legs had had a catastrophic "punch-through" on the ocean floor—a disaster that maritime engineers are careful to avoid by choosing a stable bed for their undersea footings, preferably solid rock under a thin layer of sediment. But every now and then, what seemed to be solid rock was actually a thin layer of rock over something soft—like the "roof" of an undersea grotto, which gives way under the extreme weight of the rig and collapses.

Cloyce and Glenn circled the tilted rig a few times in the plane and sighed. All the workers had been safely evacuated to the closest motel, thank God. But the rig—well, that was probably a total loss. Everything that wasn't strapped to the deck had fallen into the sea.

They landed at the closest airstrip and tried to hire a boat to see the rig up close, but they couldn't get one booked until the next morning. They were in Venice, Louisiana, population: 202—the last town on the Mississippi, out past New Orleans at the very tip of the river, but they couldn't even find a motel room. Every room in the little town was booked for a fishing tournament. Finally, they found a place to stay and took another boat to the rig the next morning. It was a disaster, literally. All of the 9 5/8" casing had spilled out of the derrick and into the sea. Everything that wasn't secured had gone in too—including some employees, but all got out safe. Glenn stared at the catastrophe and realized: Wait a minute, plenty of stuff *was* tied down.

Stuff was indoors, in cupboards, tucked away in lockers and tool cages. Glenn was not about to leave money on the table.

When Dad returned to Snyder, he called several buddies and gathered a few employees.

"What the heck are you up to, Glenn?" mused Cloyce.

"Goin' back out there in a boat," my dad responded, "and I'm grabbing everything that's not welded to the rig. We can save some inventory before it collapses completely."

Cloyce shook his head and smiled. That was typical Glenn Patterson.

When they landed, my father phoned one of the local tool pushers, who came by and picked him up in his truck. They swung by the rescue motel, rounded up some of the original crew. "Get dressed," said Dad. "We're going back out to Big Foot."

Furtive glances were exchanged between some of the men: Is he nuts?

It don't really matter. Bottom line: he's the boss. And he's going back.

It reminds me of those Saturday mornings where Robert and I were woken up to cut pipe. You groan at first. The mission makes no sense. You think to yourself: This is absurd; it's a waste of time. But Dad is unwavering, so you fall into line. You work as a team. And something magic happens.

My father took a dozen guys with him back out to that collapsing rig. The barge got them close to one leg, and they clambered aboard. They had to use safety ropes as they navigated the platform, which had tilted to 45% at this point. They grabbed anything and everything of value, from fire extinguishers to frying pans. Passing things back in a human chain to the waiting barge. Tools, spare parts, equipment. Patterson Gulf Coast had spent $225,000 on that rig, plus there was the $750,000 in losses trying to operate it—and my dad was not leaving until he salvaged all he could from the sinking platform. They crawled into the sleeping quarters, grabbed TVs, radios, walkie-talkies. They climbed into the shop to save the power tools and any drilling equipment they could find. It was precarious, exhausting. The deck was starting to get wet and extremely slippery. The crew worked until the rescue barge was packed and the sun was starting to set. Glenn, covered in grease, looked around at the haul.

Was it worth a million? Probably not. But he couldn't have tried any harder, which put him at peace. Cloyce, meanwhile, was back in Snyder, where he'd been talking to the insurance reps, who just happened to be inspecting Big Foot One when it started keeling over. They were standing on the platform in the middle of a routine inspection when the footing punched through the ocean floor. I can only guess how fast their pulses must have been racing—both on the most basic level of personal safety and also in terms of professional consequences—as Big Foot teetered precariously into the ocean. This for sure was going to be one big-ass insurance claim. Just how big-ass no one really knew, until Cloyce started hearing them talk about a "CTL." What the hell is a CTL? he wondered.

Glenn and Cloyce flew to New Orleans with their own insurance rep to meet with the salvage experts and the two insurance suits who were working the claim. They continued to jabber on about designating Big Foot a CTL. Neither Cloyce nor Dad had a clue what it meant. Finally, Cloyce had heard enough.

"What the hell is a CTL?" he demanded.

"Constructive total loss," their insurance rep replied.

"You mind giving that to us in English?" said Dad.

"It's a fancy insurance term. It means the case is a complete write-off. They issue you a check for the full amount of your policy. Two million dollars."

Glenn and Cloyce got very quiet after that. Did they hear correctly?

Two. Million. Dollars. Yup. Oughta have it within a week or so. If they declare CTL.

One day later, CTL was declared. To get the money, Cloyce and Glenn had to take their banks to Houston to sign a release of the liens on Big Foot One. When the check for $2 million arrived a few days later, Cloyce and Glenn hollered out loud and thanked their lucky stars. It would have taken years to clear $2 million off the operations of Big Foot. For a guy like Glenn who started out as a roughneck, covered in grease and paying his own way through school, that was a lot of zeros. A big damn number. He and Cloyce paid off their bank and every investor and sold the other barge rigs, and Patterson Gulf Coast was done. Just like that.

What little was left of the CTL check healed Cloyce's and Glenn's personal financial situations, thereby improving Patterson Energy's chances as well. Soon their years of acquiring deeply discounted inventory started paying off. They had parts and pieces and whole rigs to put back to work. The inventory allowed them to operate more efficiently and undercut competitors. They were soon working at full capacity.

It helped, of course, that oil prices were heading north once more and about to skyrocket. Yup. This story involves the Middle East, again—and a guy named Saddam Hussein.

Chapter 9

IT'S ALL ABOUT THE OIL, STUPID

Saddam stirred five teaspoons of sugar into his thick coffee. Arabic brew tastes like black mud unless you sweeten the heck out of it. It's thick and dark and pretty much the consistency of, well … crude oil. Oil was everything in the Middle East. As the world's fifth-largest supplier, Iraq had ambitions to increase its regional hegemony. Saddam had used his oil revenues to build up the world's fifth-largest army, with more than a million men in uniform—drafting three-quarters of his male citizens under 50 to achieve it. He had planes, choppers, tanks—everything you need to kick ass.

Saddam had started flexing his military muscles toward the end of the previous oil boom by declaring war on neighboring Iran in 1980. The war lasted eight years and ended in stalemate. Saddam had shot one of his own generals in the head for failing to advance; he'd used chemical warfare against the enemy, every bomb in his arsenal. But after eight brutal years and too many lives to count, the borders between Iraq and Iran remained pretty much as they were. The United Nations had to step in and call it a draw.

Part of the failure was Saddam's audacity in trying to swallow a bigger fish. As the world's fourth-largest supplier of oil, Iran was one notch *above* Iraq in the pecking order. The country was almost four times bigger than Iraq, with twice its population. Iran had mountains to cross and a decent-sized army of its own. But Saddam had a Napoleon complex, so Iraq duked it out for eight years with its northern neighbor, then gave up in humiliation in 1988. The Iraqi people were exhausted and demoralized. There was another problem, too: the price of oil was in the toilet. So Saddam didn't have the money to rebuild. He needed a big win. Desperately.

Thus, on the evening of August 2, 1990, Saddam looked east, where the moon was rising, finished his coffee, and gave the order to invade Kuwait. This time the Iraqi victory was swift and decisive—though that was hardly surprising. Kuwait is 25 times smaller than Iraq, with almost no army, yet it ranks right after Iraq as the world's sixth-largest supplier of oil—a pretty tempting fish for a hungry shark like Saddam.

He made public speeches in the weeks before the invasion about how Kuwait was deliberately overproducing oil to keep the prices low and hurt the Iraqi people. He also accused them of illegal "slant" drilling across the frontier to steal oil from Iraq—meaning oil rigs on the Kuwaiti side of the border had been drilled at an angle, so they were extracting mineral rights that didn't belong to them. The Kuwaitis denied the charges. But who knows? Oil is oil, after all.

That's how Saddam saw it. By seizing Kuwait, Iraq would control 20% of the world's oil—as much as the Saudis—and they'd also have a strategic seaport on the Persian Gulf, where half the oil is shipped. Did Saddam really think he'd get away with it? Did he forget that the guy sitting in the Oval Office was also an oilman?

George H. W. Bush wasted no time in assembling an international coalition to defeat Saddam. After five weeks of aerial bombardment, his army was in tatters. U.S. tanks rolled in, and it was over in a matter of days. But Saddam had ordered his retreating troops to torch the Kuwaiti oil fields. They set 700 wells aflame—raging fires that took almost a year to put out. It's extremely difficult to extinguish well fires; only a few companies worldwide are equipped to do it. Saddam's scorched-earth policy blackened the sky for months, made many coalition soldiers sick, and sent oil prices, once again, soaring. There was another backlash against "dependence on foreign oil," which meant a new flurry of domestic drilling—good news for Patterson Energy.

By doubling down on themselves and their fleet while others were fleeing for the exits, they now had a dependable company with 13 rigs and equipment to spare. With Glenn at the helm of field ops and Cloyce running things at HQ, Patterson quickly gained a reputation as a dependable company that got the job done at the price it promised. All the rigs were working. Cloyce looked at Glenn one day and said:

"Time to buy you a new suit."

"What for?" said Dad, who thought his old suits were just fine. But Cloyce had a rock-solid reason. "We oughta go public right about now, don't ya think?"

It was a no-brainer. Patterson was on a solid upward trajectory; the market was in a steady climb. Perfect time for an IPO. Glenn did not jump up and down, however. He agreed with the strategy; he just hated the idea of doing a dog and pony show in front of a bunch of bean counters, which is exactly what you have to do when you launch an IPO.

"Can't you do this without me?" hemmed my father.

"It's called *Patterson* Energy," smiled Cloyce. "They're going to want to meet us all."

Glenn presented well. He had an air about him that said: You're in good hands. Dad was the Marlboro Man, the guy who got it done. Cloyce was the consummate oilman, deal maker, and company architect. They were a formidable duo.

But Dad dreaded the idea of having to parade around a bunch of Wall Street bankers. Cloyce assured him that they could avoid New York for a while—they'd find an investment bank closer to home. He did a little poking around and came up with an outfit out of Denver called Blinder Robinson. They were the country's top penny stock brokerage firm, almost 2,000 brokers and growing fast. They'd launched plenty of IPOs.

So Cloyce and Glenn flew into Denver in early 1990. Dad was wearing a new Armani suit, and he looked the part, albeit squirming slightly. They took a taxi downtown and shot up to the penthouse of a high-rise on Yosemite Street. They never met company founder Meyer Blinder personally, but there were plenty of smooth-talking bankers with big grins and warm handshakes. They were pumped about Patterson—they're going to clean up, they said.

Blinder, himself, was an impressive guy, cut from the same cloth as my father. He was raised dirt-poor, the son of a Brooklyn candy store owner from Kiev, Russia. He had to drop out of high school to help run the store—his grueling daily hours: 5 a.m. to midnight. Then he served his country in World War II, where he stormed the beach at Normandy and won a Purple Heart after an artillery attack left his body permanently peppered with shrapnel. You could still feel the fragments in his right arm. But it hadn't stopped him one bit.

The classic overachiever, Blinder built up a series of successful businesses. He wound up in securities and finance, where he became a multimillionaire. That's where Patterson is headed, too, his team assured Glenn and Cloyce, who basically ate it up.

Never once did either of them think that Blinder Robinson didn't have the capital to back a $5-million IPO. Patterson Energy easily got their notice from the SEC to be "effective" for their IPO, meaning ready to be traded as a stock. At that time, it was a fairly straightforward process, filling out SEC Form 1, which is basically seven questions plus a couple of years' worth of financial disclosures. But the brokerage firm needed to be made "effective," too, and somehow Blinder Robinson could NOT get its SEC notice. Patterson had spent $60,000 with the firm and was getting all kinds of excuses about why the IPO wasn't happening. Then Meyer Blinder himself went bankrupt and was barred for life from the securities business. He would soon be serving 40 months in federal prison for racketeering, money laundering, and fraud. Both Cloyce and Glenn—men who prided themselves on their ability to sense a man's true character—had been screwed by Blinder Robinson.

I'd like to tell you that it was the last time that ever happened, but it wasn't. And the next time was a heck of a lot worse.

Chapter 10

PTEN

Blinder and Robinson, as it turns out, were flat broke and in no position to take anyone public. "Blind 'em and Rob 'em" went the 1987 headline from a *Forbes* article about Blinder Robinson that Cloyce and my father somehow missed. In their defense, there was no Internet—hard to do your due diligence like we do it today.

The scathing *Forbes* piece began:

ON DEC. 19, 1986 the Securities & Exchange Commission found that Meyer Blinder had committed securities fraud. As of Mar. 23, 1987 the president of Blinder, Robinson & Co. was to be banished from the brokerage business for life.

Poor Meyer. Even as the banishment order was about to go into effect, he was celebrating with a thousand of his brokers in Las Vegas. As the brokers gambled at Blinder, Robinson's annual sales convention at the Riviera Hotel & Casino, a sign in front of the casino read, "Meyer Is Back."

In fact, Meyer Blinder would successfully stall the SEC ruling in a series of appeals that wound up before the U.S. Supreme Court, including a gag order, which is why Cloyce and Glenn hadn't heard about any trouble when they approached the firm to take them public in 1992. Needless to say, the initial Patterson IPO was a miserable failure and quickly withdrawn. Dad found himself foaming about it. He had half a mind to fly back to Denver with the Patterson Beater to get back the $60,000 they'd advanced to Blinder. Cloyce decided to use legal recourse instead. They filed a criminal lawsuit to recover their advance and eventually got about half of it back.

Meanwhile, Cloyce needed to hustle and find another brokerage firm to take them public fast while the oil market was still decent. Prices had started to slide, and Cloyce was worried they'd tank. A board member and investor of Patterson introduced Cloyce to a firm out of New York City called Gilford Securities, which invited Cloyce for a meeting with one of its directors, Steve DeGroat. Dad stayed at home for this trip, leaving Cloyce to make it happen by himself. DeGroat was pressed for time because he had a very important lunch to attend that day. He met with Cloyce for exactly 30 minutes and politely listened to Patterson's story. He then asked Cloyce to leave the room while he and his associates discussed the deal. Cloyce sat in the waiting room and thought: Well, that was fast. At least he hadn't paid them $60K!

When DeGroat emerged, he had canceled his lunch. He took Cloyce instead to the Bull & Bear Steakhouse at the Waldorf Astoria in Midtown Manhattan, where they had T-bones and ribs and settled the deal right there on a napkin at the restaurant! Just the way Cloyce and Dad liked to do business.

With a listing as PTEN on the NASDAQ exchange, the 1993 IPO raised $5 million for Patterson Energy. The initial goals, modest by design, were to pay off $3 million in long-term debt and have some cash on hand for acquisitions. The timing was perfect; investors went bullish on PTEN, and the stock just took off, splitting three times over the next five years. The original Snyder investors who had bought those first unauthorized shares were given real equity, which they were required to hold for 13 months before selling. Some of them cashed in as soon as they could and earned decent money. But those who held on made small fortunes. It was a great deal for Dad and Cloyce as well, allowing them to pay down debt and go on another buying spree. But they wouldn't just be chasing rigs this time—they'd be gobbling up whole companies.

Glenn and Cloyce had studied the oil futures and saw the writing on the wall: choppy waters, which meant the market could be heading for another crash. Though their hunch proved correct, they couldn't possibly have known that within five years, the price of crude would bottom out to its *lowest nominal price* since World War II!

What Cloyce and Glenn did know, from their experience in the '80s, was that a downturn could present an opportunity. At the start of the '90s, the land-based drilling rig business was highly fragmented, with a bunch of companies about the size of Patterson, which had 13 rigs, all told—and everyone was hustling and trying to underbid each other to get the drilling contracts. Companies like these are very vulnerable in a slump and usually the first to go bust. The best defense is consolidation, which allows economies of scale and more competitive pricing.

There were a handful of big fish already swimming in the pond. One was Nabors Industries out of Houston, which had been launched in 1952 by Clair Nabors, a rare female petroleum engineer in a field dominated by men. Under her leadership, the company pushed the boundaries of drilling technology in 1963, becoming the first to drill in subfreezing conditions in Alaska. During the

'70s oil boom, they began a series of mergers, and by the '90s, they'd become the 800-pound gorilla, with more than 300 working rigs.

Jockeying for the number two spot was Grey Wolf Drilling and UTI, both with rig counts in the middle double digits. Cloyce and Glenn decided that this was a horse race worth entering—and, boy, did they go for it.

In the four years following its IPO, Patterson increased the size of its drilling fleet from 13 rigs to 46 by acquiring Questor Drilling in a $6.4-million cash and stock transaction in 1994 and then Tucker Drilling Company in 1996, among some more acquisitions. They were just getting started.

Cloyce had his eye on UTI, which was adding rigs and swallowing up competitors at about the same pace as Patterson. In fact, a number of times Cloyce had gone around to kick the tires at another driller only to find out that Mark Siegel, chairman of UTI, had been poking around a day earlier and already made an offer. They were neck and neck, constantly making the same moves.

You'd think that Cloyce Talbot, a laid-back, second-generation oilman from West Texas, and Mark Siegel, a slick Hollywood lawyer who'd been raised in Beverly Hills, might have little in common. But, as businessmen, they thought remarkably alike. It went back to the purchase of UTI itself, which had gone public in 1993, the same year as Patterson.

The company had likewise been formed a decade prior, but unlike Patterson, which began from scratch, UTI came to be when an East Coast utility spun off three subsidiaries into a new drilling operation: Union Supply Company, Triad Drilling Company, and International Petroleum Services Company—hence the initials UTI. The Philadelphia investment bank that had brokered UTI's 1993 public offering was ready, a few years later, to offer up controlling interest in the company—53% of outstanding stock.

That's when Cloyce came to take a look. The company had 27 rigs at the time, so it wouldn't come cheap, but this was a great opportunity for Patterson. Glenn and Cloyce decided to offer $3/share and flew to Philadelphia to make the proposal in person—it's always good business practice to look the other guy in the eye when you're trying to close a deal.

But when they got there, everyone was acting very strange. No one would look at them. It was weird. Finally, someone came out and said it: the company's been sold. Mark Siegel came in last night and offered $4.25 per share.

Mark Siegel? Cloyce frowned. He prided himself in knowing just about everyone in the business. Who the heck is Mark Siegel?

UTI was Mark Siegel's first foray into drilling; that's why Cloyce and Glenn hadn't heard of him at the time. Raised in Beverly Hills, Siegel had gone to law school at Berkeley, then became a rising star at a firm that advised the Disney family on their investment portfolio. Siegel, a strong negotiator with great business instincts, was instrumental in steering the Disneys to buy a controlling interest in Blockbuster Entertainment at just the right time—when those megastores were popping up everywhere like Starbucks, because renting movies back then meant getting in our cars to pick up the DVD. Blockbuster had the biggest selection by far, which made it the fastest-growing company in the sector. The Disneys ensconced Mark Siegel as the president of Blockbuster Music so he'd have an insider view of their investment. It paid off. Siegel was able to get the Disneys out of Blockbuster in the nick of time, just before Netflix came out of nowhere and obliterated it.

Siegel was just warming up. His next pivot was a bold move from movies to oil. Usually, you see that pivot in the other direction: oil money going to Hollywood, as in the case of Howard Hughes and John Paul Getty. But Siegel thought it was time to move his West Coast clients into Texas.

"I'm perhaps one of the more unusual characters in this business that's filled with unusual characters," Siegel said recently to a reporter from Bloomberg. He persuaded his Hollywood clients to acquire a minority stake in a well-servicing company that became Weatherford International, fourth largest in the world. The Disneys put Siegel on the board. "That's how I learned the business," he told Bloomberg.

And he learned it well. Cloyce quickly realized that Siegel was a competitor to contend with—Patterson's main rival. Or ... partner? They toyed with the idea of a merger, even had a few meetings in which Cloyce and Mark got to know one another. They developed great admiration for each other while remaining fiercely competitive. Both companies kept snapping up rigs throughout the 1990s, to increase their valuation. No sooner did Patterson grab another dozen rigs than Siegel would add two dozen to UTI's fleet. It was like running neck and neck—in a marathon.

By early 1997, Patterson had 87 rigs to UTI's 82, and that's when I enter the story: the moment I finally agreed—after *two* refusals—to work for my dad at Patterson.

I'd been out of school for two years at that point, having graduated from Texas Tech with a BS in biology in 1995. I thought I wanted to be a doctor at first—to get as far as I could from the oil field, just like my dad had done when he became a teacher. But I quickly realized I did not have the passion or the patience for medicine, and I was soon poking around for other options. Tonya and I had just gotten married, and I wasn't sure how she'd react when I admitted to her that I was not going to be a doctor.

The turning point came for me during my volunteer work at a county hospital, where I went on rounds with the attending physician. I remember that he was doing an intake one time where this hypochondriac patient was completely exaggerating the severity of his wounds. The guy had a couple of scratches, and he was going on and on. The attending doctor dutifully wrote everything down in the guy's chart, and I remember thinking, For God's sake, just rub some dirt on it! That's what Dad would say to us whenever we got banged up. Rub some dirt on it—meaning toughen up. I had half a mind to blurt it out to the guy in the hospital bed, which is when I looked around at the other premeds—attentive, listening, taking careful notes—and that's when I knew: I wasn't cut out for medicine.

Once while I was trying to determine my new career path, Dad said, "Why don't you come and work for Patterson?" I deflected the question with an answer about wanting to forge my own path, not be "the boss's son," which I know he respected. Robert and I had both been a "Son of a Boss" while growing up, and it had sucked. So he gave me a look and said, "Good. Because I wasn't going to hire you, anyway." He thought that response was funny, but he had been serious when he popped the question.

It had been hard to do—the first time I had said no to my dad. I'd already worked on and off for Patterson on odd jobs since my late teens. I knew exactly what was in store for me. It was always the toughest assignment and the lowest pay. Dad went out of his way not to show any favoritism. So I looked elsewhere and landed a sales position at West Texas Caterpillar, my first job out of school. It was in Lubbock, about an hour from home; I had a relative who worked there.

I went through their management training and then joined the sales force, selling used industrial engines and machinery. Most of our customers were in the oil sector, so I was "oil field adjacent." Tonya and I would go back home to Snyder on weekends; Dad would pounce and half-jokingly say something like, "You the boss yet?"

I was barely six months out of school, but Dad knew I had the desire to do more than sales. Then Glenn would come around and repeat the idea: "Why don't you come and work for Patterson?" And I turned him down. Again.

Third time Dad popped the question was in 1997. His idea was a little different this time. It was right after Patterson had acquired West-Tex Drilling, a former competitor with 30-plus rigs operating out of Abilene. Dad offered to put me to work in one of the field offices in Midland, out of the spotlight—instead of the home office in Snyder, where I'd be under a microscope. It felt like a real job offer this time. And there was icing on this cake: my mentor and boss in Midland would be Jimmy Slay, a close family friend whom I loved.

Jimmy had taken me hunting as a kid numerous times. Just him and me. He taught me how to tune into nature, how to move without making a sound. He was a man of deep faith, and I found that really inspiring at age 12. Dad was so private about his feelings about God; I honestly didn't know what he believed. He would always say, "Jesus and I have it worked out." I never knew what that meant. And here was Jimmy Slay, proud of his love for Jesus. It's something I was longing for. And that's what bonded me so deeply to Jimmy; he paved the way for my own salvation.

So I'd be reporting directly to Jimmy Slay in the Midland sales office, 90 miles away from the Patterson headquarters in Snyder— those were the terms of Dad's third (and definitely final) offer for me to work for PTEN. I took a deep breath. It was time to say yes to something both Dad and I knew would be good for me.

Tonya and I had already been living in Midland, where we'd moved for my job with Caterpillar. Now I'd spend the next three and half years selling drilling contracts under the tutelage and supervision of Jimmy Slay. I learned a ton about how to deal with people, how to treat everyone with respect. From Dad and Cloyce, I learned the intricacies of running a public company without selling your soul. Even with the acquisitions happening at a blistering pace, they still held onto their small-company principles: work hard, be fair, be honest, treat everyone the same.

Patterson was expanding so fast that they'd recently brought on a hotshot accountant named Jody Nelson to help them grow the company. They had two important acquisitions in 1998 alone. In January, they bought Lone Star Mud for just under $13 million in cash and stock, followed in February by a $42.2-million merger of Robertson Onshore Drilling with a Patterson subsidiary. Then in September came the $3.5-million purchase of Tejas Drilling Fluids. And then many more. It was head-spinning.

Now that PTEN was a publicly traded company, every deal required detailed accounting and paperwork—not exactly fun times for the duo who liked to do their deals on napkins. That's why they hired Jody Nelson. He'd been working for an outside accounting firm that was conducting a routine audit of PTEN. Cloyce saw that Jody, in his 20s at the time, was an absolute wiz with numbers and offered him a job in the Patterson accounting department, where he exceled. Glenn thought the guy was sharp as a tack. Cloyce promoted him and took Jody under his wing, made him company comptroller. Patterson soon needed a new CFO, as their older CFO wanted to retire. Cloyce thought, Why not Jody? Glenn agreed. They knew he was young, but he was also a quick study; they figured they could help him with what he didn't know. They were right. Jody's smarts allowed him to easily assume the role of CFO.

There was only one problem. Jody was a crook.

Chapter 11

MILLIONS AND BILLIONS

Their trajectory was dizzying. In one year alone, 1999, the share price surged 56%. Then it soared 87% the following year, even when the market as a whole *dropped* by 10%. The company was on fire—worth more than $60 billion, number 7 on the Fortune 500 list. I'm talking about Enron. And we all know what happens next.

The energy sector has always had its share of swindlers. With every oil boom comes some fraud—mostly in the form of bogus stock scams, tempting naive investors to bet on a surefire winner. Enron, the energy-trading giant, was an extreme example of this, where a handful of insiders made buckets of money. And everyone else lost their shirts.

Something can happen to certain people, I guess, when they start signing seven-figure checks and looking at balance sheets with 10 digits—especially when greed and cutthroat competition are part of the corporate culture. You know how Jeff Skilling treated his workers at Enron? There was a performance review panel; every year they'd rate each employee and fire the bottom 15%. Just like that. It didn't matter if someone was going through a hardship or health crisis. If you didn't make the grade, you got canned. They used to call it "rank and yank." That went along with "pump and dump." That's what they nicknamed the scheme at the top, where they'd inflate the revenue forecasts and sell their shares on the "good news."

They were all in on it: the founder, the president, the CEO, the CFO, family members. All of them willfully swindling the investing public or looking the other way and getting rich. It's very distasteful to me. Scandals like Enron give the energy sector a bad name.

When you're raised by a man like Glenn Patterson, your word is your word. That's how he ran his family, and that's how he ran his business: they were both built on trust and treating employees like family friends, getting to know them. My guess is that Jody Nelson was not a crook before he joined Patterson. That's how he managed to sneak into the hen house undetected. He was a family guy with a pretty wife and three small kids. He didn't draw attention. He worked hard.

It started small: a padded expense account, a bogus receipt. But Jody kept getting away with it, and pretty soon he just couldn't stop. It became pathological. When they finally caught up to him in 2005, the SEC would be calling it "the embezzlement case of the century."

Cloyce didn't notice a thing. Nor did Dad. Their focus was elsewhere.

Patterson was growing by leaps and bounds, embroiled in an all-out rig war with Mark Siegel. Since he assumed control of UTI, Siegel had made the strategic decision to sell all service and support assets, to focus entirely on drilling and their pressure-pumping business. That meant going head to head with PTEN for the number 2 land driller spot, after industry giant Nabors.

They wanted to crush each other—or merge. Either way, Cloyce and Glenn intended to beat Siegel to the finish line. The company with the most rigs would control more board seats and command more stocks in an eventual merger. By 1997, Patterson had pulled into the lead, with 99 rigs to UTI's 82. But Siegel kept buying up rigs until the eleventh hour.

They were scheduled to merge in February of 2001. In January, Siegel paid more than $13 million for six more rigs in three separate deals. By the time the companies were finally ready to shake hands in February, it was a dead heat: each valued at an impressive $1.3 billion, with around 150 rigs apiece. But Patterson had been only 23 years in the making, while companies that made up UTI went back to the late '30s and '40s. Cloyce and Mark knocked the whole deal out in little more than a weekend.

It was a proud moment for my father. In two short decades, the former San Antonio schoolteacher and basketball ref had cata-pulted himself to the helm of a public company worth $2.6 billion. They had agreed to make Mark Siegel chairman of the combined company. Cloyce would serve as CEO, and Glenn would be presi-dent and COO, in charge of day-to-day operations—which is where things got touchy. Even though he was now at the helm of the second-largest land driller in America with a fleet of 302 rigs, Glenn's plan was to run the ship more or less the same way he had when they had just two rigs back in Snyder—with phone calls and handshakes. That didn't always sit well with the newly derived board of directors, who were accustomed to a more corporate envi-ronment with memos, meetings, and paperwork. Total buzzkill for my dad. Even from the Midland office, and well before the UTI merger, I could sense the impending culture clash and decided this was a good time to skedaddle. I didn't want to be a potential liability for my father if things got ugly. He understood. Thought it was a good idea.

So I left Patterson in 2000, before the planned merger with UTI. I went off and formed my own company, TMP Companies. I started out with one employee and an ambitious goal. We planned to build a large oil field equipment and rig-up company. We began by assembling and rigging up industrial trailers and trucks for the oil field. For any kind of specialty equipment, we'd either build it or source it for our customers. Eventually, I started manufacturing heavy parts and equipment for both the land-drilling market and the work-over markets. It started slowly and was teetering on failure. I even had to take a second job because I couldn't afford to pay myself. I'd go in early and lay the day out for the welders and mechanics at TMP, then go to a day job as sales manager for a local fuel distributor, and then return in the evening to TMP to make payroll and pay bills. I had a great copilot named Jerry Armitage. He was the GM. We scrambled like hell to make it each month.

Dad saw the toll it was taking on me, and he hated the debt I had gotten myself into. At first, he told me the company idea was not going to make it and I should consider throwing in the towel. But as it grew, he seemed to back off some and admired my persistence. Once, he compared it all to his building of Rig One and Two, and that made me very proud.

Eventually, TMP became a successful business, and I worked it full time until the end of 2005. I had started a couple of other businesses along the way that were not so successful. My Midas touch wasn't as all-powerful as I had thought. But in late 2005, I felt it was time to sell all of my ventures and start a new oil field service company. I was actually thinking about building some drilling rigs. Thank God another mentor of mine came and talked me out of it. Ken Huseman was about to take Basic Energy Services public, and he thought I might fit in well at the growing company. He and I had become friends over the years as TMP had built some equipment for Basic. I learned a ton in my six years of running my own gig. I guess Ken saw the potential: I had won some, lost some, and been trained by some pretty smart oil field icons. I guess it paid off. I went to work for Basic in February of 2006 and eventually worked my way up to CEO.

My father had his own learning curve during those years after the 2001 merger. Good thing he enjoyed hard work, because the merger worked him like a dog. The first challenge was a brutal round of layoffs Dad and Cloyce were forced to make—slashing the staff from 7,500 to half that size in a matter of four months. 2001 was another mini crash.

Let me put this in context. Job cuts are par for the course in a merger. You consolidate and streamline to make the ship more efficient. It's the reason you merge: to be more competitive in the marketplace. So you naturally eliminate a certain number of jobs.

But the layoffs of 4,000 employees at Patterson-UTI—approved by the new board and its chairman, Mark Siegel—were draconian. There were market conditions at play, for sure. Crude prices were stagnant again, so it wasn't just the merger. Cutting staff was a smart business move, contributing, no doubt, to PTEN doubling in value over the next five years. Siegel was a numbers guy, and he was really good at it.

But Glenn was a relationships guy. It was all about the people you worked with and worked for. You got to know them. That's what made it so tough for him to hand out around 4,000 pink slips in 2001. In the end, he knew it was the right move too.

Glenn and Cloyce had prided themselves on keeping layoffs to a minimum during the downturns. They'd talk to the staff personally and propose temporary pay cuts (starting with their own) so they could afford to keep as many employees as possible in the Patterson family. That's what made Dad a great boss. It was all about camaraderie and relationships. He liked to get in there with the guys on every job when he could. He took the time to visit each rig—and not only in a crisis, when disaster strikes and choppers come zooming in from everywhere. Dad liked to visit a rig when things were gliding along without a hitch so he could slap some backs when the employees were feeling good about themselves.

But, as the PTEN rig count hit triple digits, this got harder and harder to do. After the merger, it was impossible. It became quickly apparent to Glenn that the only way to manage a fleet of 302 rigs was to hire really capable VPs, superintendents, and tool pushers and delegate decision making into the field. It's ultimately more efficient. The boots on the ground can see and solve a problem a million times faster, cheaper, and better than a guy back in the home office. So you hire guys you like and trust. And you give 'em a long leash.

It's sort of what they did with young Jody Nelson, now CFO of Patterson/UTI, a company worth billions. On any given day, there was a pile of invoices to pay, which meant dozens of wires, hundreds of checks—routinely six figures, often seven. Under Cloyce and Glenn's supervision and with UTI's former accountant, John Vollmer, on the board and assisting Jody too, everyone felt he could handle the load.

But that's just when Jody's stealing got out of hand.

Chapter 12

IT HAPPENED RIGHT IN FRONT OF US ALL

Things just exploded after the merger.
Consolidated income at PTEN doubled in 2001, jumping from
$513 million to $990 million. Net income quadrupled to $164 mil-
lion. Then, during the two-year market downturn that followed,
they turned to page 1 of the Patterson Playbook: buy more rigs and
build some newer versions. In the five years following the merger,
PTEN added almost a hundred rigs to its fleet, now just shy of 400
strong. The headlines at the time read: "Patterson-UTI Earnings
Soar" and "Patterson-UTI Profits Triple." With the stock skyrocketing, the board of directors approved a doubling of their dividend
in 2006 to 32 cents a share.

Yet that's the year my father resigned as president of PTEN.
Dad had been tired for years. He had wanted a way out, but business
had just been too good and running too smoothly, for the most part.
The UTI merger had been closed, and it integrated and blossomed
under Glenn and Cloyce's supervision. It was nothing less than a
smashing success. 2006 was a great time for Dad to retire. Just one
problem—the CFO was found to be a crook, and everyone was
blindsided. It took almost another full year to get through the Jody
saga before Dad could resign.

Though this was not spoken overtly—not in public, anyway—the Jody Nelson scandal must have played into Dad's decision. He had a front-row seat to one of the largest corporate crimes in American history and, unfortunately, got to be part of the story.

Jody's malfeasance had been stunning. It worked like this: He had set up a phony shell company called XIT Land and Energy in Lubbock, which would invoice Patterson for equipment and services. Payment would be made by wire to the XIT account at the Bank of America in Lubbock, controlled, of course, by Jody. He cranked out fake invoices from XIT by the dozens for parts that were never shipped and services that were never rendered—tens and hundreds of thousand dollars' worth on any given day or week. There were hundreds of invoices, all told.

In 2001 alone, there was a mind-boggling total of $7,650,000 paid by Patterson to XIT. The following year's total jumped to $8,550,000. Jody was constantly covering his tracks and keeping XIT out of any kind of spotlight. By 2003, he was authorizing more than $15 million in fraudulent invoices. A single wire transfer in 2004 clocked in at $2,126,891.25, paid to Aero-Space Reports for a Beechcraft King Air, a turboprop private plane for six passengers and two crew—just one of several luxury aircrafts that Jody bought for himself with Patterson money. Jody didn't even bother to funnel this one through XIT. He just pretended it was payment for a seven-year maintenance contract for a Patterson-owned plane and recorded it in a journal entry that way. He used fake copies of signatures to back up the authorizations.

So why didn't anyone notice it? Not staff, not senior management, not professional outside auditors (in their review of all corporate books required annually for a publicly traded company), not Glenn, not Cloyce, not John Vollmer, not Mark Siegel? No one saw anything out of line because Jody covered his tracks very carefully, and he played everyone well. The folks who did ask or should have asked questions were reassured and given enough work and distractions that they shrugged it off. Jody was a master flatterer as well, and he could lay it on thick enough to get someone off their guard. Plus, people generally liked the guy! He was nice and charming and fun, always ready to listen or help financially with any cause. And he was a great thief. As for those above him, be it management, auditors, or board, he always had the answers—*almost* always, as it turned out.

No sooner was a wire sent than Jody would go into the books and recode the transaction to a different vendor. So XIT was largely kept off the ledger. This cover-up happened hundreds of times. You'd think one of the Patterson/UTI internal accountants—there were six of them, at this point (reporting partly to Jody in his role as CFO)—was certainly going to catch this.

Jody, who's no dummy, was prepared for that. In fact, his plan was diabolical. He had multiple schemes to claim that reasons for these invoices were necessary.

One of worst involved *me*—and my relationship to Dad.

This happened a couple of times, I later learned. One of the firm accountants would be going through the ledger and notice a discrepancy. The original invoice said XIT, but the books were coded to a different vendor. They'd bring it, as they ought, to the attention of their boss, Jody, who'd, surprisingly, take full responsibility for it.

"I did that," he'd readily admit. But he had an explanation: "Glenn asked me to."

And that was usually that. Jody was playing into the fact that everyone loved and trusted Glenn. If Glenn asked Jody to do something, there was a damn good reason for it. But if there were lingering suspicions, to stop the discussion in its tracks, Jody might lean in and whisper, "It's something involving Roe."

That one makes my blood boil. Jody was making it seem like there was sketchy, or at least close-to-the-vest, business going on between me and Dad—something that he'd asked Jody to cover up. The implication: "It's secret Patterson family business that we don't ask questions about." So the subject was quickly dropped. And Jody kept stealing.

He started spending, too. He acquired a 19,000-square-foot mansion in the heart of Lubbock, along with other properties, three luxury motorhomes, 35 motorcycles, 10 airplanes, boats, Jet Skis, a cattle farm—he even bought a damn airport. And he was just getting started. Jody wasn't outright flaunting his wealth, but he wasn't exactly hiding it, either. I remember my father saying, "Beats me where Jody gets his money." Dad assumed like many that his wife's family was wealthy, which helped Jody with his cover.

The funny thing is Jody could have gotten away with it. He would have snuck off scot-free if he'd done the one thing he was incapable of: stop stealing. I've had this conversation with Cloyce, who agrees. If Jody had just stopped after embezzling $40 million or so and lain low—doing nothing sinister for two years and two audits—he could've turned in his letter of resignation, and no one would've been the wiser. Hardly anyone goes back beyond two audit cycles, particularly when a company is skyrocketing and everyone's happy.

But Jody couldn't stop; he just wanted more and more. That was his illness. All the way until 2005, when, finally, the game was up.

An internal auditor eventually decided to go over Jody's head to report something funny to the board. It was petty thievery compared to the millions that Jody had embezzled —and nothing to do with XIT. In the end, what tripped up Jody Nelson was a relatively minor padding of an expense account. A junior auditor brought it to the board's attention: Jody had been drawing $2,000 a month in an expense account he was not reporting.

As a way to abscond with funds, it was pretty clunky, especially when you compare it to his slick XIT scheme. I think Jody had put it into motion years earlier, probably the first money he bilked from Patterson-UTI, and he'd forgotten about the fact that it was still running on auto in the background.

Mark Siegel called Cloyce about it, and Cloyce confronted him about it in fall of 2005. Jody couldn't very well blame it on my father or me or anyone else this time. So he came up with a different excuse, probably thought up on the spot.

"It's that commuting expense you agreed to," he explained swiftly, suggesting that Cloyce had approved $2,000 a month paid to Jody toward mileage and vehicle wear and tear, when Cloyce had agreed to pay for Jody's commute to Snyder from his home in Lubbock until he could find a weekly residence in Snyder permanently.

Though Cloyce had no memory of the conversation, he was still willing to give Jody the benefit of the doubt. But that didn't mitigate the problem. Whether a legit expense or not, the problem remained that Jody should have ended the practice years earlier and had never reported the expense correctly. He sure hadn't turned in any receipts or paperwork. It was $24,000 a year over four years, almost a hundred grand. If Jody were trying to frame it as a "non-accountable" expense account, he'd have been obliged to report $24,000 as income subject to withholding.

It wasn't a one-time oversight. It had been going on for years. Not the behavior or actions of a CFO.

"I'm sorry, Jody," said Cloyce. "We gotta look into this hard. The board will have to meet and discuss this, and we may have to let you go. In fact, I'm almost sure we will."

Jody nodded silently—probably relieved as hell that Cloyce was firing him, thinking that he had bilked one-tenth of 1% of what he had actually stolen from PTEN. So he quietly packed up his office on November 3, 2005, and got the hell out of Dodge.

That night he wrote the following group e-mail to his 65 staffers at PTEN:

"I really just wanted to express my complete and humbled appreciation to each and every one of you. As I look anxiously on to the next chapter of my life, I cannot help but feel as though I am leaving what has been an incredible family to me. Each of you share something very very special and that is your place here at Patterson. Enjoy it, cherish it and give it and its people all you have and I promise you that you too will walk away one day better for it. I have loved this place for almost a third of my life and hope that you are able to take from it the same things I have … security, friendship, family and pride."

I almost feel bad for him. Here he was, writing his goodbye letter in one of his mansions, surrounded by gaudy possessions purchased with stolen funds, fleets of motorcycles, artwork, tapestries. Typing about all the things he had at Patterson: "security, friendship, family and pride."

Feeling sheepish, I bet, and lonely as hell, he was singling out his top staffers for special thanks, and then Jody closed with a nod to his bosses, who were copied on the e-mail:

"Cloyce and Glenn you have always been risk takers … and you surely took one with me many years ago. You entrusted me with your beloved company and I hope someday that I can repay you for this opportunity. You have been more than bosses to me ... mentors and fathers always personifying hard work, integrity and fairness. Thank you.

"I will miss you all ... Jody"

He was feeling vulnerable and scared as hell, I'm sure. It was only a matter of time before someone discovered another irregularity in the books, one that would lead to the XIT mother lode.

It took less than two weeks, in fact.

Within days of Jody leaving, someone came across paperwork suggesting that Glenn had authorized the purchase of a company called Arrow Construction—in other words, making an acquisition unilaterally, without telling Cloyce, which was way out of character.

"Ain't that your signature?" asked Cloyce, pointing to the bottom line of the authorization for expenditure, where Glenn had ostensibly gone rogue and greenlit a $1.5-million acquisition. It was his signature, all right—but Glenn had no memory whatsoever of the transaction. Both of them realized it at the same time: Jody. Then another accountant walked into to Cloyce's office to ask about a vendor: XIT.

Cloyce said, "We don't have a vendor named XIT."

Glenn was consulted. Nope, no vendor by that name.

The accountant dropped his head. "I was afraid you'd say that."

"Why?" asked Cloyce. "What have we spent with them?"

"Millions" was the response.

No one could believe it. How? How the hell could this be happening? The answer again was painfully obvious: Jody.

It had to be. He'd used a special laser copier, the Justice Department would later disclose, to get Dad's signature onto the AFE.

This was suddenly much bigger than a padded expense account. This was embezzlement and wire fraud.

In came the FBI, with a team of forensic accountants. They combed through every line of the Patterson ledger and quickly found a string of criminal activity. Patterson issued a press release on November 14, making the embezzlement public. Three days later, Jody turned himself in to U.S. Marshals, who froze all of his accounts. They seized his homes, cars, furnishings. In all, he had stolen approximately $78 million over an eight-year period. It is still one of the worst embezzlement cases in U.S. history.

Glenn was in a state of shock. The idea of thievery on that level was completely foreign to my dad. He couldn't fathom why Jody had done it. He kept shaking his head and saying: "We did and would've kept making him a very rich man—the *honest* way. He didn't have to steal anything." Jody's starting salary as PTEN comptroller was $200K, plus another $300K in bonuses and stock options. Not bad for a kid barely out of his 20s.

He was still young enough when apprehended, in fact, that they remanded him to house arrest—with his *parents*. Jody was arraigned on January 3, 2006, by U.S. District Judge Sam Cummings on two counts. The first count alone, willful certification of false financial reports and aiding and abetting, could've landed Jody in jail for 20 years with a $5-million fine; the second count was wire fraud and aiding and abetting, which came with a $1-million fine and up to 30 years in prison. When the judge asked the defendant for his plea, Jody replied, "Not guilty."

What a complete son of a bitch—to have the absolute gall to say that in open court when he knew the jig was up! A few months later, Jody had the good sense to change his plea, and sentencing was scheduled for October 10, 2006. Judge Cummings called the court to order and asked Jody whether he wished to address the court before sentencing. He was much more contrite this time.

"I am truly sorry and ashamed of my betrayal," he said. "I know words are cheap for me, but I want to apologize to the board, the management, and the employees."

Even more than Cloyce and Glenn, the hardworking Patterson employees were furious about what Jody had done. "Nelson stole more than money," said John Vollmer, who had replaced Jody as CFO. "He stole an unblemished reputation."

Then it came time for sentencing. Judge Cummings began with a brief statement: "We are at a crossroads in American society where corporate malfeasance has appeared to reach an all-time high." He cited the cases of WorldCom and Enron. "This type of conduct simply cannot be tolerated in our society," said the judge. Then he handed down the sentence: full restitution, through seizure and auction, of the $78 million that Jody stole—plus 25 years behind bars. No parole.

Glenn and Cloyce felt the punishment was just.

U.S. Attorney Richard B. Roper made a brief statement outside: "I'm very happy with the sentence Judge Cummings imposed today on Mr. Nelson. I don't recall ever seeing a case in this district that involved more greed than that displayed by Mr. Nelson. He deserves every one of the 25 long years he will serve in federal prison."

The court mandated a live auction to sell off all of Jody's toys at a huge event in West Texas. I wanted to go see what the master thief had assembled, but Dad and Cloyce warned the whole family to stay far away from it all. They didn't want any of that stuff, and they didn't want any of their family involved. I wish I could have gone. My friends who went said it was massive: classic cars, new cars, motorcycles, RVs, helicopters, planes, tractors, ATVs, Jet Skis, boats, guns, arcade games, antiques, paintings—you name it; Jody had bought it. He had hidden his biggest splurges, but he had lived like a king, buying and hiding assets all over the country. They even auctioned off some ranches and other properties. All told, they collected several million dollars that Patterson-UTI received after the feds took the full corporate tax rate off the top. Yep, the feds considered the income to Patterson-UTI to be ordinary short-term gain, and they were there to collect their share first. The money Jody had generously loaned to many different people and companies all had to be accounted for too. Some of those people were crushed by what Jody had done. The repercussions seemed to never end.

PTEN stock, which had lost nearly one-third of its value that year, rose 2.4% on the news. I wish I could say that Dad felt vindicated, but I think he just felt sad: sad about Jody ruining his life, sad for Patterson-UTI, and sad that this mess happened while he was partly in charge. He felt he had let everyone down. Some would say Glenn and Cloyce's leadership after Jody's arrest was some of their best. They picked the company up and got everyone back to work. And Patterson-UTI did very well in the following months and years. Dad waited until the dust settled to retire, but it was not the ride into the sunset he had probably hoped for.

At the time of Jody's sentencing later in the fall, Dad had been officially retired for six full months. And it was really getting to him. This was a guy who never took a vacation—not once. A guy who worked weekends—both Saturday and Sunday. The exception to this was Vegas. Dad figured if you're going to take time off work, you may as well go to Sin City, but, eventually, it lost its allure. Dad would mostly spend weekends in the Patterson yard, or at our little farm in Blackwell, where he was born, or out at his small farm near Snyder. He loved to plant a garden. But a Glenn Patterson garden was always about three acres! I think you get the picture.

There was constantly something to do, something to fix. When he was working full time, he had clients to call. Problems to solve. Asses to chew. Pickups to wash.

Taking time off was simply not in Dad's playbook. And here he was—*retired*.

It was almost a four-letter word.

But there was something else gnawing at Dad that was even more troubling. It was subtle. But he couldn't deny it anymore. He had started forgetting things.

Chapter 13

GOD AND
I HAVE AN
"UNDERSTANDING"

I noticed it, too. So had Mom. The man with file cabinets in his brain—who never forgot a phone number, who remembered everyone's birthdays, even the secretaries', and who even knew the names of their kids—was starting to lose it.

I remember playing golf with him one Saturday afternoon. It was a gorgeous day, and we were having fun. We were hypercompetitive, of course, and playing for money, as always. Five bucks a hole, I think it was. But here's the thing. Dad started losing track of the bet, which was so unlike him. I remember being shocked. He had always been a whiz at mental math. He'd always had a *calculator* in that brain of his, tucked alongside those file cabinets.

"So I'm up five," he said at one point on the front nine.

"No, Dad," I corrected him. "I'm up five. Remember? I won the last two."

He squinted. Then he tried to make light of it. "Just testing you," he mumbled, almost to himself, as he climbed into the golf cart.

I remember thinking, "Hmmm." Then it happened again. I got concerned.

145

Mom had been seeing it for some time. Robert saw it too. He and I had discussed it many times. We convinced Dad to see his doctor, which he did. Dad was troubled, like we were, about how he was feeling mentally, but he thought it could be a bug or a chemical imbalance, meaning something treatable.

When they told him "early-onset Alzheimer's," he wasn't buying it. Dad just wasn't ready for that. Then he tried for a brief period to embrace it. So, at first, he told us about the diagnosis and said he was going to take the doctor's orders and exercise, eat right, and stave off the disease. That didn't last long, and then the next thing I knew, he was saying he may have had a stroke. He would say the lapses in memory might have even been caused by some chemical he was exposed to in his early years in the industry. Whatever, but he didn't say Alzheimer's anymore. And if you ever brought that up, he would correct you fast.

So he started running, biking, and working out like crazy. For a while that worked, but the disease progressed. He got lost on his bike once, and that scared him. So he went to some more clinics and got the same answers: Alzheimer's. I'm telling you: he would have none of that talk. It was strange—a stroke he could accept, but Alzheimer's? No way. I guess some people recovered from strokes, and he wasn't ready for what he thought was a death sentence with Alzheimer's.

I believe that God has a plan for all of us. And that Dad's Alzheimer's, as cruel as it may have been, was part of the Lord's plan for him: allowing Glenn—or forcing him, really—after 60 years of almost nonstop work, to slow down.

It was time to introspect.

What an amazing run he'd had: from his impoverished roots in Blackwell and Ira and paying his way through school to building a business from scratch, surviving two downturns that leveled the competition, and creating considerable wealth not just for himself and his family but also for his employees and shareholders. Dad had also found time to be a husband and a father, and now he was a granddad, too. Tonya had given birth to our kids, Nathan and Anna Grace, who were now in kindergarten and preschool; my brother, Robert, and his wife, Angie, had had three kids, Chandler, Logan, and Jenna. But Dad was not quite ready to settle into the role of Patterson patriarch. He wasn't at peace just yet. I could sense it when we spent time together.

Who could blame him? The prizefighter who'd hung up his gloves had just taken the beating of his life. Three blows to the gut in rapid succession. First there was the Jody disaster, with its still-churning feelings of anger, disappointment, and guilt. Then there was his unceremonious exit from Patterson, which had left him feeling empty and incomplete. And now there was this enemy from within, Alzheimer's. They all hit him in basically the same period of his life.

No wonder he wasn't at peace. I did a lot of praying for him that year. So did Mom and Robert. We asked the Lord to help open Dad's heart. But everyone is responsible for their own salvation. You can't make the horse drink. Especially a stubborn mule like Glenn Patterson. I can count on one hand the number of times that Dad came to church with us growing up. It was so rare. I remember those moments vividly.

Dad would be sitting next to me in the pew, towering over me because he's 6'4" and I'm nine. It was Easter. Dad sang along in his baritone but mumbled the words so badly that you couldn't make out even one. He stood when he was supposed to stand, sat when he was supposed to sit, and he prayed. I watched him from the corner of my eye only to find him peeking at me out of the corner of his. I'd even catch him saying "Amen." But it wasn't coming from a place of conviction. He was just doing what was expected of him—like he did when he was a boy.

Glenn didn't hate going to church growing up, but he didn't love it, either. Mostly, he was grinning and bearing it, just like he did when he came with us. "God and I have an understanding," he'd tell my mom. He had the same words for me and his close friend Jimmy Slay if we ever brought it up.

But then he'd be curious at night when Mom took out her Bible. She was deeply devoted to her Bible study—she still is. She'd sit at the kitchen table and open the Good Book regularly. Glenn would often come ambling in, fishing in the fridge for a snack. He'd watch her for a moment. Thinking.

"You really believe all that stuff?" he'd ask. Genuinely curious.

Janeen would nod sweetly. "I do."

Glenn would shrug and shake his head, not totally getting it. He knew there must be something to the Bible. People he respected had a deep connection to scripture, including Mom.

"What is it that you and Jimmy have that I don't have?" Glenn asked my mom one evening. "Y'all always seem so ... so ... happy."

"It's because we believe," replied Janeen. "We know what's going to happen to us."

"Well, I want that, too," declared Glenn. But he wouldn't do anything about it. He certainly didn't show up in church with us. Sunday was a day to work. And if that was caught up, you played cards or golf.

Dad had this misconception, I think, about what it means to open yourself up to God's love. He thought it involved surrendering to an external authority—giving up control. Glenn felt that the act of surrender to God implied weakness, and he'd never given up on himself, not once. I guess he thought that if he put his faith in God as opposed to in himself, he'd lose his mojo or he'd have to release something that he desperately wanted to keep. He didn't realize that salvation is a gift. You just have to accept it. The only thing released is your old self.

This was my path and my experience. God is within us. He's the voice that's always been there, guiding us in our journeys as humans—whether we listen to him or not. I still fight it today, but at least I know what I'm pushing back on. Dad felt that he'd toughed it out until then on his own and that no one had his back but his own tenacity and self-drive. If God was helping, it was only to help stiffen the resolve he already had. It was up to Glenn Patterson to help Glenn Patterson. If God existed, he was busy doing things for other folks who needed it more than Glenn Patterson.

But here's the irony. My father had heard—and heeded—that voice numerous times in his life. It had told him to marry my mom, to follow her to college, to go back to the oil field, to help others in need, to "loan" money knowing he'd never see it again, to be kind, to be honest, to be fair no matter the costs, and countless other times. Dad would call them hunches, or gut feelings. I'd say they were moments that God spoke to him and through him—where his will aligned with divine will and miracles happened.

But there was hardship, too. He sinned and made mistakes like anyone. Sometimes big mistakes. He also experienced brutal challenges during his life. Times when God was asking Dad to surrender and just let him help. And now Dad was facing the hardest thing he'd ever been through: the feeling of his mind slipping away from him.

In moments of lucidity, which were becoming less and less frequent, he'd well up thinking about it. He knew he was up against something that was going to win and beat him in the end no matter how hard he fought. He was broken. That's when God finally melted all the ice of pride and ego. He found Glenn Patterson in need. Right where he wanted him.

* * *

The catalyst for Dad to start attending church was his old high school pal Donnie Newman, who was now born-again—and truly happy. Dad had known Donnie his entire life, and he knew that Donnie was not into religion. He was the last guy you'd see in church. Sunday was for the pool hall or the racetrack or work—at least it was back when they were the defiant duo in high school. But then Donnie shipped off to Vietnam and came back different.

He never talked about the specifics of what happened over there. Donnie wanted those memories to be erased from his mind. But it changed him, according to Mom and Dad. He was never quite the same after that. Donnie was often withdrawn, broody, tormented.

Dad and Donnie had supported each other at every opportunity they could during their lives. They had worked together for Patterson and played golf, and they had an unspoken friendship their whole lives. Dad had seen Donnie through some really dark times, so imagine how refreshing it must have been for my father to see Donnie smiling again.

He was low-key about what had happened at first. But Dad wanted to know. So Donnie told him he'd been going to church. He had walked into Cavalry Baptist Church as a somewhat stranger to God, not unlike Dad. But little by little something happened during the sermons. And finally Donnie was saved.

"I can't explain it," shrugged Donnie. It was like a weight had lifted, and it made him want to go back, again and again. Pretty soon Donnie, at age 62, decided to get baptized, and church became a big part of his life.

Dad was intrigued.

In 2009, Mom and Dad attended the wedding of Donnie's daughter at the Cavalry Baptist Church. Donnie made sure to sit Glenn next to Preacher Larry McAden at the lunch reception. Glenn really liked the guy, as Donnie knew he would. Larry made everyone feel welcome, a warm personality, clearly beloved by his parishioners. Glenn looked around. Everyone had smiles. Everyone was happy.

What the heck? thought Glenn. What do I have to lose? He began attending church. Little by little it must have sunk in. He decided to get saved and baptized. He was having trouble getting the words out to my mother, but she understood what Dad wanted, and so did Donnie. Donnie took Dad to meet with Larry McAden about what it meant to be saved and baptized. He understood and was willing to surrender to God, accepting his gift of grace by confessing Jesus as his savior. He wanted to let go of the old Glenn and become the new. I was very excited for him, and I wasn't alone.

Mom, who was a Methodist and had not been baptized as an adult, elected to join him. On the day of the ceremony, Dad had chosen to be baptized in a private setting. Not the norm, but Larry had agreed. Glenn wanted Donnie and his wife, Shirley, to attend, but no one else. Dad told Mom that he wanted to wear his jeans and boots to be baptized in. She laughed and said it would be OK to wear them to the church but he should probably change into some shorts under his baptism gown. That did not set well with Dad, and that's when she knew it was so important to him. He wanted to look his best for God. Pastor McAden let people wear whatever they wanted to be baptized in, but he persuaded Dad that the shorts under the gown were fine. He took three steps down into the baptismal font, took Larry's hand, and professed himself a Christian.

It took all of Larry's strength to dip Glenn's towering frame backward and submerge him in that water. He came up blinking but with a big grin on his face. He was overjoyed.

Mom asked him, "How do you feel?"

"Great!" he said.

Mom went next, and then they hugged, dripping wet with tears of joy.

When Dad's baptism was announced in church the following Sunday, he stood up. He thought he was about to head down and do it again with a full church this time. His apprehension gone, he was ready. Mom quietly sat him back down and explained it was only the announcement. I'm so proud that he was so proud.

When Dad accepted Christ, he won the fight of his life. Glenn became the Christian he was always meant to be. God was patient and waited for the right moment to break Dad and save him all at once. And Glenn knew he was blessed. He knew that not everyone gets that kind of chance.

When Dad started attending church, he was amazed at how everyone treated him so well and was so nice to him. People were generally happy to see Glenn Patterson in the pews. Mom said their little area in Calvary where they sat every Sunday got more and more crowded. She felt like Dad's attendance sparked a small revival. After all, if Glenn Patterson thought church was important, then a few other crusty old farts could make it there, too. Dad was humbled at how warm and welcoming the church was toward someone like him, even when he'd never made it a priority in the past.

My mother caught him weeping in bed one night. She rushed over and said: "What's wrong, Glenn?"

Dad turned to her with tears in his eyes: "I'm sad that I have just now found God."

She put an arm around him and reassured Glenn, saying that God had a beautiful and mysterious plan for all of us, and that it's never too late to connect with him. She reminded Glenn that his own father, Monroe, had opened himself to God literally in the final moments of his life. My mother had been an eyewitness to this extraordinary eleventh-hour conversion. She had told Glenn this story back in 1980, when it happened. But Dad hadn't really taken it in at the time; he didn't have a personal connection to it. But now he was all ears.

So Janeen retold Glenn what happened with my grandfather on his deathbed. Monroe had been diagnosed with terminal lung cancer and was in the hospital in Snyder. He wasn't doing well and was not expected to live long. Family members, including my mom, were taking turns sitting at his bedside in shifts. Mom happened to be on call when a preacher from a small local Baptist church showed up to visit with Monroe. His name was Buck Hackfield. Buck sat down and made some small talk with Monroe, and then he got down to brass tacks: "Monroe, you got something to say?"

Monroe replied, "Yeah, Buck, guess I do. Guess I can tell you as good as anyone." He cleared his throat: "Are there things I regret doin'? Hell, yeah ..."

"You're not talking to me, Monroe," Buck stopped him. "You need to talk to Jesus."

That's when Janeen stood up and said, "I should probably go while y'all visit." She got her things to leave, but Monroe stopped her: "No, you stay. You should hear this."

He knew Janeen was a devout Christian. He wanted her support in this moment. Monroe turned his eyes back to Buck. "What do I say?"

Buck answered, "Just talk, Monroe."

He did. Monroe confessed his whole life right there and right then. Buck led him in a prayer of salvation and acceptance of Christ. He was saved on the spot. Mom cried, Monroe cried, and even old Buck cried.

When Monroe's wife, Eudell, returned from her break to relieve Mom, she saw that she'd been crying and asked her why. They stepped outside into the hall, and Mom told her everything. No one could believe that Monroe had accepted Christ. Mom said, "Eudell, it was beautiful. You should have been here and not me." But Eudell just smiled and said, "No. It happened just like God wanted it to."

"And that's the way it was with you, too, Glenn," Mom told my dad. "God waited until you were ready to accept him."

Dad nodded solemnly. Mom smiled at him. "When you die, Glenn, your father will be waiting for you in heaven." Glenn's eyes welled up. But these were not tears of sadness. He was joyous at the thought of seeing his father again.

"I'm ready to see him," Dad said after a while. But it would be years before he did.

Then he looked Janeen in the eyes. "There's no fixing what's wrong with me, is there?" It was one of the few times my mother says my dad ever really faced his illness.

"No," she said gently. "I don't think God intends to heal you. For whatever reason, this is his will for you." Glenn took it in stoically. His faith was now strong enough to accept God's will fully. He knew he was no longer in charge—and would never be in charge again. Never really had been in charge at all. What a relief.

Chapter 14

SING A SONG, GRAB SOME SHOVELS, AND GET BUSY

Dad never wanted a big memorial service.

Was he proud of his life? Sure. But in a quiet sort of way. It was the pride that comes from being able to look at yourself in the mirror and know you've shown up with your A game. Consistently. Dad had faced his challenges with dignity and tenacity but also with grace. Never losing heart. Always willing to try a different tactic. He would have made a great quarterback.

But he didn't need or want the spotlight. He preferred to deflect the attention to others. Well, those "others" really appreciated him. They turned up in numbers for Dad's memorial service, which took place on Saturday, June 27, 2015, at 10:00 a.m.

It felt like half the town showed up at the First Baptist Church. I was sitting in front with Tonya and the kids, feeling nervous. It was almost my turn to speak. I had worked hard on my eulogy, hoping to do justice to my father's life.

He'd lived his final years in relative tranquility in a condo unit of Raider Ranch. He was a decent patient. He had good days and bad ones, but he was as comfortable as we could make him.

He'd tease his caregivers, joke and laugh, even when he lost his speech. He'd get mad, feel bad for behaving badly, then forget. He always loved sweets and always kept his pride. But somewhere deep inside he had some peace that I could see. His faith in Christ had changed him.

I visited him every chance I had. Tried to play cards a few times, but even that was getting too confusing for Dad. We'd just talk or sit together. Sometimes we prayed. After a while he became more distant, and usually I would just talk, or Robert would. When Dad got real bad, Robert and I had to go see him together because it became so emotional. We relied on each other to manage the visit. Robert was better than me at talking to Dad. He could get Dad laughing. He couldn't speak but just a few words, but he understood when Robert would tease him. I got him laughing a few times too. It was a great feeling.

When we would leave, I'd fly back to Fort Worth, where I had moved Basic Energy Services, and Robert would head back to work in Lubbock. Both with tears in our eyes.

Dad's death hit me a lot harder than I'd imagined. I had thought, foolishly, that I already said goodbye in a sense when we lost him to Alzheimer's; it felt like I'd been grieving for years. But there was this finality to the moment when I heard the news that he'd passed. It was just devastating. Dad had been such a big part of my life.

Less than one week later, the grief still strong, I steadied myself to address the crowd at the memorial. Brother Larry McAden was presiding—the same preacher who had officiated six years earlier when Dad had been baptized. I was glad to have Larry there.

This time was so damn sad. Dad was about to have his sixty-ninth birthday. Too young. Many in attendance at his memorial were shocked, given how indomitable Dad's spirit was. As a Christian,

I knew that Dad was with the Lord. But my heart was still heavy, and I was worried about losing my composure when I took the podium. As a company CEO, I give plenty of talks to large crowds. But this was different. This was my family, community, kids, nieces, nephews ... Mom. She was as choked up as I was.

"Hang in there," whispered Tonya. She was praying for me. I looked at my kids. They smiled encouragingly as Larry McAden summoned me to the pulpit. "Now a few words from Glenn's youngest son, Roe Patterson."

I rose to my feet and felt eyes glued to me as I made my way up.

It took me back to 2008, when Dad won the Top Hand award at the banquet of the Permian Basin Petroleum Association. That was two years after his Alzheimer's diagnosis; he'd started slipping. But no one knew about it outside the family. We were worried silly as he took the stage to give his acceptance speech. Would he get disoriented and tongue-tied? Would he become paranoid? Make a fool of himself?

I prayed. Mom prayed. Tonya prayed. Robert prayed. And somehow Glenn pulled it off with flying colors. Witty, gracious, and to the point. When he came back to the table, he gave us one of those looks: What's everyone so worked up about?

He was a real clutch player, always rose up in the key moments.

I felt the emotions getting the better of me when I began to speak at the First Baptist Church. But I thought of Dad and realized suddenly he was not remote. He was not gone. He was *with* me. It calmed my nerves. I took a breath and began:

Many people have had the opportunity to know Glenn Patterson over the course of his life. If you knew him, you probably called him a friend. To Robert and me, he was just our dad. He was many things to many people. He had a way of leaving a lasting impression on everyone he met. There were many ways to describe Dad:

He was friendly and kind. Dad rarely met a stranger, he always liked a hard worker, and he rooted for the underdog every time. He loaned his money, his time, his advice, his possessions, and the shirt off his back to just about anyone who asked. Getting paid back never seemed to be as important as the feeling he got knowing he helped someone.

He was competitive, tough, prideful, and yet humble. I've never known anyone who liked to compete more than Dad. He could turn anything into a contest, and he loved to win, whether in business or in a footrace. You couldn't beat him at any wager or game because he demanded a rematch if you did win, and you knew that "double or nothing" was the next thing coming out of his mouth. He was tough beyond measure. And took great pride in all he did. He was proud of his company, his fellow employees, and his family. But he was humble all at the same time, passing the praise to anyone but himself when there was praise to be had.

He was fun, quick to laugh, quick tempered, and tough to please. Dad loved to laugh and always loved a great joke. Though he told few, he laughed at most. He loved a great practical joke even if the joke was on him. But he had a temper too. And if you ever saw it, you never wanted to see it again. For those of you who actually saw that little white foam of spit gather in the corner of his mouth, well, then, you are in good company, because many of us saw that spit and knew we were in for it. He was tough to please, but he passed out plenty of "attaboys." He always wanted you to do even better.

He was sometimes shy; he was honest and ethical. Dad never liked the limelight of any kind. He would hate what we are doing right now. He would say, "Sing one song and then grab some shovels and get busy." He was honest to a fault and hated a cheater or a liar. He would say, "Fight 'em fair," and then with a grin he would jokingly say, "But if that ain't working, try cheating a little." But he never cheated. He didn't mind getting an edge on you, but he wanted you to know it when he did.

He measured people by their heart and their integrity— never by their great deeds, their money, and especially what they said. To him you deserved respect when you accomplished much and asked for no recognition or repayment. You just did what was right and necessary.

And finally Dad was a Christian. But for most of my life he was not. I knew he wanted me to know Christ, but he wanted very little relationship with God for himself. He didn't come to church with us, and we didn't talk with him much about God. When we did talk about it, he would say, "God and I have an understanding" and "Don't worry about me." But I did worry. I worried I wouldn't see him in heaven. You see, it was pride that prevented him from being saved, and we knew it, and he knew it. It wasn't shocking. I've known many men who suffered from the same problem. In fact, we all probably have. He felt that if he gave into Christ, he would be giving up that part of him that never gave up, never surrendered, and never quit fighting. He didn't realize that the fight had already been fought, and it was an overwhelming victory; he won, and he never had to do anything but accept it.

Then he became ill. He knew he was up against something that was going to win in the end no matter how hard he fought. And he was broken. And that's exactly when he accepted Christ and won the fight of his life. He became the Christian he was always meant to be. God was patient and waited for the right moment to break him and save him all at once. And he knew he was blessed. He knew not everyone gets that kind of chance.

I believe his legacy and his testimony should be this: it is never too late for Christ, and it's never too early. Dad was a good man and a great dad. But he had many flaws, just like we all do. And he was a sinner. He wasn't perfect, but because he was broken and believed, he is perfect now.

Epilogue

HARD WORK

Basic Energy is one of the largest oil and gas well-servicing companies in the nation. I joined its ranks in February of 2006 as the VP of corporate development. That July, crude oil hit a mini peak of just under $80/barrel, before plummeting 20 points by November. But that was nothing. In 2008, the drop was more than 100 points. It's been up and down for a decade, and it's still volatile.

All that time, I did what I've always done. It's what I learned from Dad—keep to the job at hand, play fair, outhustle the next guy.

They promoted me to senior VP in 2008, then to SVP/COO in 2011. Every time I visited Dad during those years, he'd tease me and ask the same question: "You the boss yet?"

"Not yet, Dad," I'd reply.

"That's cuz yer not hustlin' enough," he'd say. "You gotta work harder."

I'd smile and promise: "I will, Dad."

One visit in May of 2013 was particularly special and amazing all at the same time. It was right after Basic's board of directors had officially named me as the new incoming CEO. I flew to Lubbock for a regular visit and ended up talking with Dad by myself for a while. By this time, the Alzheimer's had progressed substantially, and he was under 24-hour care. He would try to talk some, but he mumbled and was rarely understandable. While I never knew whether he fully comprehended the conversation, I decided I would share my news of becoming CEO with him. After all those years of teasing, I figured he would want to know.

He was staring out the window as I cleared my throat and said, "Dad, they named me CEO of Basic. I guess I'm gonna be the boss after all."

He snapped his head around and looked me right in the eyes. He did it so fast it made me jump back a bit.

For a moment he just stared. Then he said, "Good boy."

He said it so clearly and directly that I was left speechless. I hadn't heard his voice like that in over a year. No mumbling at all.

After he spoke, he just nodded a little then turned to stare out the window again. I was so shaken by it I couldn't talk without a lump in my throat. I managed a few more minutes of idle conversation, and he just mumbled something and stared out the window. When I got in my rental car to leave, I could barely hold back the tears. I couldn't believe how he had just spoken and clearly understood me. What I had said had been important to him, and for a split second the veil of Alzheimer's was gone. He was lucid. I had made him pleased, and that pleased me.

Dad never spoke to me again. Not like that. Eventually, I felt he had forgotten that I was his son. That was tough. But we had that day in May of 2013, and that meant everything to me.

I really miss him. The decisions I've had to make as Basic CEO have been tough, to say the least. I would have loved his counsel on a few of them. After I took the reins at Basic in 2013, the market cap of Basic Energy Services (NYSE: BAS) took off over the next year and a half to around $2 billion. In 2014 we reached a record revenue of $1.5 billion, and our earnings before interest, tax, depreciation, and amortization (EBITDA) reached a record at more than $300 million. We grew the company by leaps and bounds and employed almost 6,000 people. I was named 2014 Top Fort Worth CEO for Publicly Traded Companies by a local magazine and appeared on CNBC's *Mad Money* with Jim Cramer twice in 2014. It seemed like everything we were doing was improving the company's performance each day. Dad used to say that a drunk monkey could run an oil field service company when oil was high. He was right.

But I also inherited more than $800 million in debt—one note worth $475 million issued in 2011 and a second for $300 million from 2012, plus some leases. Easy enough to control with more than $300 million in EBITDA but a high hurdle if the oil business was to ever crash.

I remember what Dad used to say to me and Robert back in Snyder: "Rack up too much debt and you'll be scratchin' a broke ass."

I knew I had to get that debt off our balance sheet or at least reduce it. But by the time we were approaching the time frame to pay the bonds down, the oil market was in free fall, due to overproduction. It had started falling hard in August of 2014, but no one including me could foresee what was on the horizon. By autumn, the poorer members of OPEC called for a meeting to cut production in order to stabilize prices. But Saudi Arabia, the 800-pound gorilla at the table, didn't like the idea. In fact, the country proposed quite the opposite. It has always been more interested in market share than the price per barrel. So it opened the spigots, causing a free fall that lasted for two and a half years—a price drop of more than $80 per barrel. It has been the worst crash in oil field history on a relative basis. Bar none, the worst. Our stock took a beating at Basic; so did our bonds, which is where we really became vulnerable. There's a shadow market in debt that follows the stock market, and if you're not a player in the financial world, you'd never know about it. It works like this. Bonds issued by a public company can be traded just like stocks, which means that when the market is bullish on the company, those bonds get traded at a premium. A solid company is less likely to default on its debt, which lowers the risk. So $1 worth of debt could be traded up to $1.05 or $1.06, especially if the bonds offered a favorable interest rate. That's how it was during my first year or so as CEO of Basic. It was a good company with a solid management team, so our bonds were trading at a premium.

Then came the crash of Thanksgiving 2014, when OPEC raised production— exactly what Dad had faced three decades earlier, when barely a few years into Patterson Drilling, the market turned on him and he had to take drastic measures. But they just had a handful of rigs at that point. It was a much smaller operation. That's why he was able to round up my brother and me to cut pipe on Saturdays so we could make an interest payment on his bank loan. Almost 30 years later, Basic Energy Services had about 425 well-servicing rigs, 1,000 water trucks, and more than 400,000 hydraulic horse power of frac and pumping equipment at Basic. We had almost 6,000 employees—and we were all looking down the barrel of a bazooka. No more easy drunk monkey cruise control. The real work was starting.

Drilling rigs stacked out, our well-servicing rig work began to dry up, our frac crews were idle, and our cash on hand was becoming more and more precious by the day. We made our interest payments on our bonds, but we couldn't keep it up forever. Our bonds were heavily discounted at this point, trading at 60 cents on the dollar and moving lower. That's when the vultures start to circle.

Sophisticated traders are always on the lookout for deeply discounted bonds that they can scoop up in numbers to gain leverage over a company like ours—one with solid fundamentals and a great track record but at the mercy of a market downturn. By buying up all or most of the outstanding debt when a company is on the brink of default, they can dictate terms, which usually means trading the debt for equity and/or forcing the company into a restructuring through Chapter 11 bankruptcy, where, as the first- or second-position creditors, they'd be entitled to the lion's share. One way or another they end up taking over the company. And page 1 of the "Distressed-Debt Takeover Playbook" is to push the company to the brink, drain all cash, and force drastic cuts across the board. That means yard closures, good folks laid off, wages drastically reduced. I felt sick to my stomach at the prospect. It was not the Patterson way. But I was running out of options. I had an obligation to Basic's shareholders, but the employees *are* the company.

Bankruptcy seemed like such a failure. Though I knew my largest peers were going to file, I just hated the thought. But that's all I had. Patterson had managed to avoid it through two crashes. What would Glenn do? I wondered. Then it came to me.

He would save as many jobs as he could and face the bankruptcy with vigor. What if we decided to fast-track the whole process? If we prenegotiated terms with our major creditors and got as proactive as possible, it could allow us to speed through the bankruptcy process at a lightning pace. If I drove the process rather than our creditors, I could fight to keep as many of our employees on the payroll as possible.

So we sat down with our creditors and started some intense negotiations with them. It was grueling and took all of my focus— like high-stakes poker at the final table. I had only a small amount of leverage. My job was the only real chip I had. They wanted the management team to stay, and they wanted me at the helm. We had a proven track record, and we were in the best shape of all of these companies that were caught by the crash. But I had to threaten to walk multiple times. It wasn't until I actually told them I was done that we got anything done at all. I was offering them a bird-in-hand deal. If we didn't come to terms, they could be at the mercy of the court-appointed trustee, who could force them to accept something less favorable or worse: watch the company free-fall into Chapter 7 liquidation. They also had to worry I might walk away and manage to take some leadership with me.

In the end, they had all the real cards because our equity value had fallen so hard, cash was getting very low; meaning I and the original shareholders had very little ground to stand on. The negotiations were dragged out as long as possible, squeezing the cash and limiting all options. By offering to quit, I had called all bluffs and thrown myself under the bus at the same time. I hope the original shareholders will someday know how hard we all fought for them. After the smoke cleared (and the bondholders had backed the bus up and ran me over a few more times), we eventually worked out some common ground and closed a series of deals. Our CFO, Alan Krenek, was an all-star. He had never been through anything like this either, but he navigated it like a seasoned pro and kept his team focused. Our operations guys did super as well by keeping the company rolling smoothly every day. I could not have asked for a better team to be in the foxhole with. I also had a great lawyer named Ray Schrock with Weil, Gotshal & Manges, LLP. I doubt we would have accomplished much without Ray because I probably would have told the other side to stick it and walked out. That wouldn't have helped anyone. Ray kept me focusing on the endgame: save as many jobs as possible. Dad would have approved.

When enough ducks were in a row, on October 25, 2016, we filed for Chapter 11 bankruptcy. The judge agreed to fast-track Basic Energy's restructuring because we had already come to terms with creditors to reduce our debt load. We also filed a series of additional motions with the court that requested the authority to continue normal operations, pay our bills and maintain staff. I was determined to continue paying salaries and providing employee benefits without interruption during the restructuring. The judge agreed. He saw that we knew what we were doing.

We had also reached out to all of our partners and suppliers prior to filing to ensure that business could continue uninterrupted. The market had started to rebound, and I wanted to get our crews back to work. They did. And I visited them in the field, where I slapped some backs and told them to hang in there. We were in this together. If we toughed it out, we'd emerge from bankruptcy stronger than ever. And we did.

Basic emerged from bankruptcy on December 23, less than two months after filing. We now had more than $125 million in new capital, and our debt had been reduced by around $800 million. Most importantly, we salvaged around 3,300 jobs. And we're back on a growth trajectory, leadership team fully intact. Our advisers (Moelis and Alix Partners), along with Ray and his team at Weil, had helped us pull off a very difficult objective: a smooth bankruptcy. Never thought I'd brag about that one. But it could have been much worse.

All told, in retrospect, I believe this expedited bankruptcy was the only decision for Basic. I think Dad would have agreed. I spent some time after he passed thinking I'd never hear his voice again. But the truth is I've internalized his voice. That's what a good dad is, I guess. He becomes an internal barometer for you, whether he's around or not. Even more importantly, I had the most important

Father with me as well. My faith in Christ was the most incredible source of strength during the restructuring. God never gives you more than you can handle.

On April 7, 2017, Tonya and I co-chaired the Alzheimer's Association 16th Annual Memory Gala in honor of Glenn, and this is what I said to the assembled crowd:

"My dad taught me that honesty and integrity are everything in business and in life. He always said the decisions you make are only as good for you as they are for everyone you work with. ... If something is bad, it is bad for everyone. If something is good for you, it has to be good for everyone who works with you and for you—employees and customers and vendors. We all share in the good and the bad, and if we do that, business is easy."

My hope is that the Glenn Patterson approach to doing business spreads to other companies. He showed you don't have to be a cutthroat son of a bitch to do well in the oil field—or any field, for that matter. There is plenty of room for decency, integrity, and trust. That was and is the Glenn Patterson way of business, which, in the end, is an extraordinarily Christlike way. I believe that's exactly what God wanted.

You see, Glenn was a Christian-in-waiting, and he was already living many aspects of the Christian life well before he was ever saved. I'm not sure he ever understood why until he was saved. At that point, it all made sense. Even to a man with full-onset Alzheimer's. No, he was not perfect. He sinned like we all do. But it took his sickness to show him that even though none are worthy, because of Christ's sacrifice, all can find Grace. If it took diseases like Alzheimer's and Lewy body dementia to bring one man into heaven, then I have to say it was all worth it.

Christians all have their own paths to Christ and salvation. Glenn's story is just one picture of just one path. But it should remind all of us that Christ is waiting for us to accept the gift. And he is patient. He can wait a lifetime, but it shouldn't take that long. It should happen today. All it takes is death to self and one prideless act of faith. That seems like a good enough reason to write a book: so one example of faith can lead others down the path.

At least I kept it short, Dad.

About the Author

T. M. "Roe" Patterson is a 23-year industry veteran in the oil and gas services business. He was promoted to president and chief executive officer of Basic Energy Services (Basic) in September 2013 and was recognized as the Top Public Company CEO by the Fort Worth Business Press for 2014. Prior to his recent appointment, he served as the company's senior vice president and chief operating officer from 2011 to 2013. Patterson began his tenure at Basic in 2006 and has held multiple positions in executive leadership since joining the company.

Patterson's roots are grounded in the oil and gas business. He grew up working for his father in the family's business, Patterson Drilling Company. After earning a Bachelor of Science degree from Texas Tech University, Patterson joined West Texas Caterpillar for a year before rejoining Patterson Drilling Company as a contract/sales manager for its Permian Basin Division. After four years he left Patterson to form his own manufacturing and oil field service company, TMP Companies, Inc., until he sold in late 2005 and joined Basic's management team in early 2006.

Roe and Tonya Patterson have two children and reside in Fort Worth, where they are active in their local community. Roe serves on the Tarrant County American Heart Association Board, and he and Tonya were co-chairs of the AHA Heart Ball in 2016. They were also honorary chairs of the 2017 North Texas Alzheimer's Association Memory Gala in Fort Worth. In his free time, Roe is a business speaker. His speaking engagements have taken him around the country, speaking on his own personal business experiences and the practical approach to leadership that his father embraced.